THE NEW YORK RED PAGES

THE NEW YORK RED PAGES

A Radical Tourist Guide

By
Toby & Gene
Glickman

PRAEGER SPECIAL STUDIES • PRAEGER SCIENTIFIC

New York • Philadelphia • Eastbourne, UK
Toronto • Hong Kong • Tokyo • Sydney

Library of Congress Cataloging in Publication Data

Glickman, Toby.
  The New York red pages.

  Includes index.
  1. New York (N.Y.)—Description—1981–   —Tours.
  2. Historic sites—New York (N.Y.)—Guide books.
  3. Radicalism—New York (N.Y.)—History—Miscellanea.
  I. Glickman, Gene. II. Title.
  F128.18.G57 1984   917.47'10443   84-2157
  ISBN 0-03-069786-7 (alk. paper)
  ISBN 0-03-069784-0 (alk. paper)

Published in 1984 by Praeger Publishers
CBS Educational and Professional Publishing
a Division of CBS Inc.
521 Fifth Avenue, New York, NY 10175 USA

456789 052 987654321

Printed in the United States of America on acid-free paper

Preface

One day several years ago, on a summer trip out West, we passed a road sign in southern Colorado that read "Ludlow." We knew that the town had been the scene of a bloody massacre during a miners' strike in 1914, and we stopped to see whether the event was still remembered. It was indeed—we found a monument erected by the United Mine Workers of America and in a niche at its base a memorial book in which visitors, some of them descendants of the murdered miners, had written moving statements. The caretaker was an old man who, as a child, had been an eyewitness to the attack. We spent the day talking with him about this all-but-unknown fragment of American history.

After several such experiences—searching out little-known places or coming upon them by chance—we realized that often what interested us as tourists was not to be found in standard guide books. They were sending us to the holy relics of Important People; we were hunting for the battlefields and hangouts of the oppressed and the rebellious. Convinced that we were not unique, we decided to write this book, taking our home town as our subject.

The New York Red Pages is arranged as a series of walking tours that will take you to famous addresses and infamous lairs, memorable but unmarked sites, and some places where nothing remains but a good story.* Undoubtedly we have made some mistakes here and omitted things that should have been included, and we invite readers to send us corrections and suggestions:

c/o Editorial Department
Praeger Publishers
521 Fifth Avenue
New York, NY 10175

---

*There is so much to be said about Lower Manhattan that we decided to end this volume at 14 Street. We trust our readers will follow us northward in a subsequent volume, to demonstrations in Union Square and urban removal at Lincoln Center.

Acknowledgments

We would like to thank some of the many people who helped bring this book to life.

Malcolm Keith, our first editor, gave us critical and kindly support. His assistance was a crucial factor in shaping the book.

Philip Nicholson helped two amateur historians organize and clarify Chapter I. He also read the entire manuscript and made many useful suggestions.

We received numerous insights and a great deal of information on the Lower East Side from Louis Katzowitz, on Black history from Mark Naison, on architecture and city planning from Tom Jones, and on NYU from James Paul, and were privileged to be offered the vivid recollections of Annette Rubinstein, Morris U. Schappes, Carolyn Slaski, A.N. Weinberg, and Morton Sobell.

Gilbert Schrank, Caoimhín Ó Marcaigh, Ann Hickey, and Elizabeth Kahn read and commented on portions of the manuscript. In addition, Ann and Elizabeth test-walked some of the tours. The book is enriched by their observations and reactions.

We would like to thank the workers in the many progressive organizations we visited for taking the time to talk with us and give us literature about their activities, especially the people at the Tamiment Library, Liberation News Service, and Cityarts. Cityarts' overworked staff generously offered their assistance in selecting photos of its murals, and LNS, with almost no staff at all, turned us loose in their files.

We are grateful also to Ann Glickman for creating a readable manuscript out of a mess of notes, and to Willie Helmreich, Liz Mestres, Liz Macklin, Bea and Ron Gross, Gus Reichbach, Franklin Siegel, Ed Sagarin, Steve Hyman, Brian Kahn, and Paula Kahn for their technical advice and assistance.

For their moral support and encouragement through the long gestation and birth of this project, we thank our friends Linda and Philip Nicholson, Richard and Ruth Panken, Jim and Susanne Paul, and Phyllis and Marty Albert.

We thank the New York Marxist School for sponsoring a series of walking tours based on the material in the book, and Diane Neumaier for responding so enthusiastically to our request for photographs.

And finally, we wish to express our gratitude to Rachel Burd at Praeger for her patience and persistence in getting the manuscript ready for publication, and to Lynda Sharp, our editor, for believing in this book and making its existence possible.

Contents

*To our children Adina, Ann, and Miriam, and to
the memory of Tecla*

THE NEW YORK RED PAGES

Greenwich Village

East Village

Lower West Side Civic Center

Lower East Side

Financial District

EAST

1
Capsule History of Lower Manhattan

There is evidence that the eastern seaboard of what is now the United States has been inhabited for at least 10,000 years. At some point during that time, the Algonquian culture came to dominate the area. Within this large group were many tribes, related to each other by language, tradition, and social organization. Within the tribes were bands, each made up of several extended families. The bands were governed by a sachem and a council, and each by custom inhabited a particular territory. The Manhattan band lived on the southern third of the island, fishing and farming in the warm months, moving to nearby hunting grounds in the winter. To them, human beings were a part of nature, no different from the other animals that inhabited the earth, or the corn and beans, the water, sky, and land. They conducted their lives with respect for nature and their place in it.

The beginning of the end of this life came in the form of a boatload of Dutch and English seamen and their captain, Henry Hudson, who sailed the *Half Moon* into these waters on September 2, 1609. They were on a fact-finding mission for the Dutch East India Company, searching for a sea route to the fabled East. Hudson had started from Holland on a northeasterly route, but his crew grew mutinous in the freezing waters off Russia, forcing him to turn around and seek an alternative route. (He seems to have had a predilection for icy waters and steamy crews. Two years later under similar circumstances, his crew unceremoniously dumped him into a dinghy in Hudson Bay and he was never seen again.)

Hudson failed to find a way through to the Pacific, returning with a hold full of beaver skins instead of spices. So the Dutch East India Company renamed itself the Dutch West India Company and went into the fur business. In 1624 the colony of New Amsterdam was established and became the hub of the New Netherlands trading network.

New Amsterdam was a company town with a touch of feudalism. Settlers were obliged to:

Obey Company officials

Belong to the Dutch Reformed Church

Live where they were assigned

Help erect public buildings

Turn over all export goods to the Company, which exercised a trading monopoly

Inform the Company of discoveries of valuable commodities

Sell no handicrafts

Trade exclusively with the Company

Keep strangers in ignorance about Company matters

Stay away from New Amsterdam after their service was completed unless given permission to return

Cultivate the land according to Company dictates

Deal justly with others and keep their women and children on the straight and narrow*

As far as the Dutch were concerned, there were "good Indians" and "bad Indians." The good ones were those who were useful to the colonists as trading partners; the bad ones were those who resisted land-grabbing. The real estate takeover began in 1626 with the "purchase" of Manhattan for 60 guilders. Since the concept of land as a commodity was alien to the natives, they understood the "sale" as a land-use agreement in exchange for gifts. Their fatal mistake was that they expected the Dutch to remain for a time and then move on. When they realized that the colony was permanent and their source of sustenance was being stolen from them, they fought back and were driven out or killed.

The Dutch were unable to savor their new colony for long. By 1674 they had lost it to the British, who dubbed it New York, after the Duke of York, who had been given it by his brother, King Charles II. During the following century the port of New York became central to the British colonial system, the hub of trade in raw materials, manufactured goods, and enslaved human beings.

Those slaves who were not shipped elsewhere became the underclass of a highly stratified society. At the top were the large landowners—old Dutch patroons and the English beneficiaries of royal largésse. In the

---

*Adriaan Barnouw, "The Settlement of New Netherland," *History of the State of New York*, Vol. I, (New York: Columbia University Press, 1933).

middle were a burgeoning mercantile class, artisans, and small farmers. At the bottom of the heap were the indentured servants and slaves.

The latent class struggle between the Royalist Tory landowners and the Whig merchants and artisans sometimes erupted violently and dramatically. Such was the Leisler Rebellion. During the hiatus between the reigns of James II and William and Mary (1688 to 1689), New York was without a governor. The merchants and artisans of the city, taking advantage of the confusion, installed Captain Jacob Leisler as interim governor. Two years later, when the landlords recaptured power, Leisler was tried and executed for treason.

Another eruption occurred when John Peter Zenger was brought to trial. The governor, who was intent on suppressing Zenger's anti-Royalist newspaper, concocted a charge of seditious libel against him. The jury found he had written the truth and acquitted him. The Leisler Rebellion and the Zenger case foreshadowed the broader struggle that broke out in earnest during the 1760s—landlords and officials lining up with the British and most everyone else becoming part of the revolutionary movement.

In 1763 the British Parliament passed the first of a number of repressive laws that galvanized the Americans into increasing militancy. These laws were evidence of the inability of the British mercantile system to cope with the dynamic growth of the American economy. New York became one of the centers of resistance. In rapid-fire order critical speeches became demonstrations, riots became military engagements, resistance became revolution.

New York spent the entire Revolutionary War under British occupation. With the American victory in 1783, the Tories' strutting ended abruptly, and most of them fled ignominiously to England or Canada. The revolutionaries did what all victorious revolutionaries do: they seized power and expropriated Tory property.

After the Revolution, New York was the seat of the federal government as well as the nation's commercial and financial center. Freed from the fetters of British mercantilism, ambitious young men of means began inventing American capitalism. By the turn of the century they had organized the beginnings of a banking system, a stock exchange, and an insurance industry. By 1825 trade with the Orient, as well as with Europe, had been established. In that same year, the Erie Canal was completed, linking the granaries of the Middle West with New York.

The nineteenth century was marked by an enormous increase in the city's population. As New York's commercial role grew, great numbers of laborers were needed to build houses and roads, to load and unload ships, to distribute food and clear garbage. The first wave of immigrants, German and Irish, came in the late 1820s and 1830s; along with the slaves freed by New York State in 1827, they became New York's first mass work force.

Most of these workers crowded into tenements on the East Side, while Greenwich Village, to the west, became the residence of the gentry. The southern tip of the island remained its financial district.

The working class had made sporadic attempts to organize, even prior to the Revolution. But in 1829 a new beginning was made in the form of a Working Men's Party, which lasted for almost a decade and even elected some of its candidates to the state legislature. It was led by George Henry Evans and Thomas Skidmore. Here are some excerpts from Skidmore's *The Rights of Man to Property*, published in 1829, when Karl Marx was eleven years old:

> All men should live on their own labor, and not on the labor of others.... I would give the same rights of suffrage to the red man, the black man and the white man.... woman, as well as man, is entitled to the same right of suffrage....
>
> The Steam-Engine is not injurious to the poor, when they can have the benefit of it.... If it is seen that the Steam-Engine is likely to greatly impoverish, or destroy the poor, what *have* they to do, but TO LAY HOLD OF IT, AND MAKE IT THEIR OWN? LET THEM APPRO-PRIATE ALSO, in the same way, THE COTTON FACTORIES, THE WOOLEN FACTORIES, THE IRON FOUNDRIES, THE ROLLING MILLS, HOUSES, CHURCHES, SHIPS, GOODS, STEAMBOATS, FIELDS OF AGRICULTURE ... AS IS THEIR RIGHT.

In response to the same desperate conditions that gave rise to the Working Men's Party, the Democratic Party, through its Tammany machine, diverted the workers from a radical path by setting itself up as the defender of the poor. The immigrants provided the votes; Tammany provided patronage and protection, while collecting a little graft on the side.

The outbreak of the Civil War provoked mixed reactions in New York. Mayor Wood and some other Democrats advocated secession to form a "free city," but the mass of the people supported the war effort, volunteering for the army and for nursing duties. However, as the war dragged on and conscription was imposed, resentment grew among some of the white poor. It was directed against the rich and the Blacks: the rich because they could buy their way out of military service, and the Blacks because they were seen as the cause of the trouble in the first place. In five days in July 1863, the city was nearly devastated by an orgy of rioting. Mobs attacked the property of the rich, the hated draft offices, and every Black they could lay hands on. However, the majority of New Yorkers remained firmly opposed to slavery and loyal to the Union cause.

In the last third of the century, millions of poverty-stricken immigrants from eastern and southern Europe arrived; labor unions began to coalesce and the socialist movement developed; Tammany's corruption reached new heights with the Tweed Ring. The immigrants crowded into the East Side, while the homes of the rich in Greenwich Village and elsewhere in the city were showcases of ostentatious wealth. New York became the most important eastern terminus for the great transcontinental railroad system, which carried commodities eastward for export and sale and opened the Middle West for industrialization. With the invention of the elevator, the city began to take on a vertical dimension; skyscrapers rose, each vying with the others for supremacy in size and grandeur. The completion of the bridges from the Lower East Side to the city of Brooklyn, beginning with the Brooklyn Bridge in 1883, laid the groundwork for the consolidation of Greater New York, which took place in 1898.

The rapacious growth of capitalism during this period created extremes of wealth and misery. Liberal reformers devised means to help the poor while making use of the "excess" profits of the rich. The era of philanthropy began, with the establishment of settlement houses, health care, and social services to ameliorate the conditions of poverty. Under pressure from the socialist and labor movements, legislation was enacted leading to the demolition of some of the worst slums, the tightening of building codes, and the improvement of working conditions. Political reform movements were periodically successful in routing Tammany from City Hall and cleaning up city government. However, many of these improvements were only temporary.

By the turn of the century, the flood of immigrants had started to overflow from the East Side into the hitherto sacrosanct precincts of Greenwich Village. As the rich fled farther uptown to escape the great unwashed, their elegant homes were converted into low-rent rooming houses. Upon this American "left bank" converged a new kind of immigrant. From all over the United States would-be artists, dissatisfied with provincial life, came to New York seeking kindred spirits. In the first decades of the century, Greenwich Village became the center of avant-garde and left-wing journalism, literature, art, music, dance, and theater. After World War II the Village turned fashionable again. New York University started to sprawl, buying up buildings to house students and faculty; rising young professionals discovered the area; rents soared. Greenwich Village became an upper-middle-class enclave. The artists who could no longer afford the Village moved south into converted factory lofts and east into low-cost tenements, attaching new names to these neighborhoods: SoHo and the East Village.

A new wave of immigration broke upon the Lower East Side in the postwar years. The poverty and lack of work in Puerto Rico forced many islanders to uproot themselves to seek a better life on the mainland. A large number settled in the Lower East Side, where they joined some of the descendants of earlier migrations: Ukrainians, Poles, and Jews. At the same time, many new Chinese immigrants arrived, crowding into an already packed Chinatown and overlapping the borders of Little Italy. During the 1960s the northern part of the Lower East Side acquired a new name—the East Village—as the hippies started to gather around St. Mark's Place. The unemployed or marginally employed writers and theater people who live here now are in many ways the spiritual descendants of these flower children.

Since the beginning of the century, the area between SoHo and the Lower East Side has grown into a huge complex of city, state, and federal offices. It has come to symbolize both the presence of government in the lives of the people and the nature of justice in a class society. These courtrooms, jails, and government offices are the arenas in which the larger social and political conflicts are played out in microcosm. While the laws are always unequally applied to the rich and influential and to the poor, the powerless, and the political dissident, it is rare for these day-to-day confrontations to reach the eyes of the public. But on two occasions these buildings became public theaters, and the eyes of the entire country were focused on them. It was here that the state of New York staged the Criminal Anarchy cases in 1919 and 1920, in the wake of which hundreds were jailed or deported. In the 1950s the communist trials and the red-hunting congressional investigations took place here, leaving a trail of shattered careers and personal lives, and paralyzing the movement for a decade.

The appearance of the Financial District has changed considerably in the past 80 years, beginning with the construction of the early skyscrapers and culminating in the World Trade Center megaslabs. More significantly, the role of the Financial District has broadened. It has grown from being the center of the U.S. economy to being the hub of the world economy, reaching its peak immediately after World War II. While much of the rest of the industrial world had been devastated by the war, the U.S. industrial base was untouched. While the old colonial empires were disintegrating, the U.S. neocolonial empire was being formed. All capitalist currencies were pegged to the U.S. dollar. It was to be the "American Century," but it was all over in 30 years. Since Vietnam, U.S. imperialism has lost some of its teeth. But the old shark is far from dead, and "Wall Street" continues to signify money and power to the rest of the world.

Lower Manhattan is a place of contrast and contradiction. Parts of it are utterly still when the computers and typewriters stop at five P.M., while there are whole neighborhoods that are never silent, day or night. Great banks, courts, and skyscrapers overlook flophouses and ancient tenements. Mandarins of power and wealth conduct the world's business a stone's throw from the poor and struggling. This potentially explosive mix of the symbols of ostentatious wealth and the reality of grinding poverty is what infuses Lower Manhattan with excitement.

In little more than three centuries, what was once a tiny Dutch outpost has become a world capital. Each era of New York history has left its mark on the city. As you walk the streets, you will find the past hidden within the present, and the hidden present within the familiar and famous landscape that is New York.

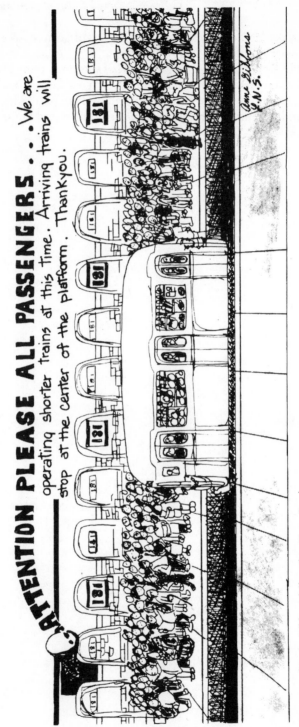

ATTENTION PLEASE ALL PASSENGERS . . . We are operating shorter trains at this time. Arriving trains will stop at the center of the platform. Thankyou.

Anne Gibbons
L.N.S.

Courtesy of Anne Gibbons/Liberation News Service

2
Practical Matters

Manhattan is a long and narrow island. "Downtown" is to the south and "uptown" to the north. Going east-west or vice versa is "going crosstown." Most of the island is laid out in a grid, with the avenues going north and south and the streets going east and west. However, the southernmost part of Manhattan, which is also the oldest, was constructed prior to the development of the grid; hence, the street arrangement here is irregular and somewhat haphazard.

The quickest mode of transportation is the subway. There are three lines: the IRT, the BMT, and the IND. They interconnect at many points and free transfers are possible at these points. We have correlated our walking tours with subway stops. We suggest that you pick up a free subway map, which is available at most token booths. Try to avoid the subways during the morning and evening rush hours (from about 7–9:30 A.M. and 4:30–7 P.M.), when they are uncomfortably crowded. And try to avoid them late at night, when they are uncomfortably empty and may be dangerous to your health.

Another way of getting around is by bus. Most follow either a north-south route or a crosstown route. While they are slower than the subway, their advantage for the tourist is that they provide a kaleidoscope of city sights while allowing the weary legs to rest. It is possible to take a bus to the tour starting points. You must have exact change to board a bus—$.90 at latest writing. A free bus map may be obtained at: Times Square Visitors Center; Columbus Circle Visitors Center; Penn Station—Long Island Railroad Information Booth; Grand Central Station—Conrail Information Booth.

Unless you are a masochist, do not drive. From Here to Eternity accurately describes the space-time warp of Manhattan. And when you arrive (if ever) you will not be able to park. If you must sample this urban madness, take a cab and let the cabbie suffer. That way you will lose only your money, not your mind.

Each of the following chapters covers a relatively small area of lower Manhattan. Every chapter contains more than one tour, and each tour has a letter name (A, B, C, etc.). Within the tour the items along the route are numbered consecutively (A1, A2, A3).

We have not gone into great detail about restaurants, shopping, and the like. For information on these subjects we refer you to the following paperbacks, which are available at most bookstores:

AIA Guide to New York, by White and Willensky. Excellent architectural commentary on practically every building of interest in the city.

Arthur Frommer's Guide to New York, by Faye Hammel. Good general guide, especially for cheap hotels and restaurants.

Lower East Side Shopping Guide, by Telzer and Greene. The only one of the Manhattan shopping guides to concentrate on the Lower East Side—detailed practical information about specific stores.

Underground Gourmet, by Glaser and Snyder. A budget restaurant guide, not totally dependable as to quality, but the odds are you will be satisfied.

The best sources of information on films, plays, concerts, exhibits, and so forth are the newspapers, and the most complete listings are to be found in the *Village Voice*. In addition, many left-wing parties and groups put out their own papers, most of them weeklies. These are available at various newsstands, especially in Greenwich Village. The *Guardian* has a good section on local events.

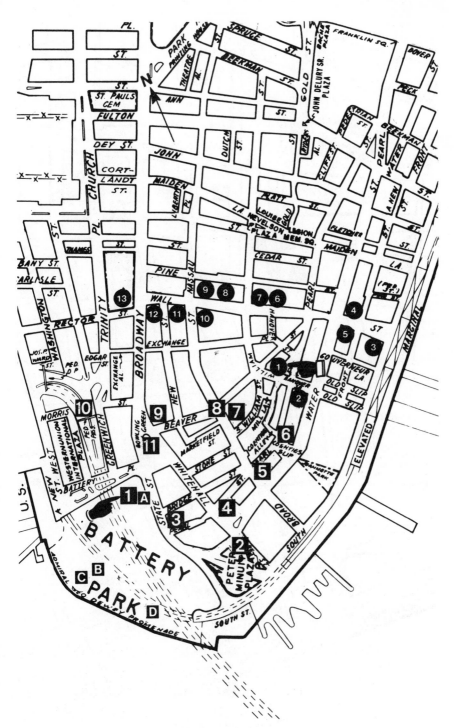

TOUR A / TOUR B

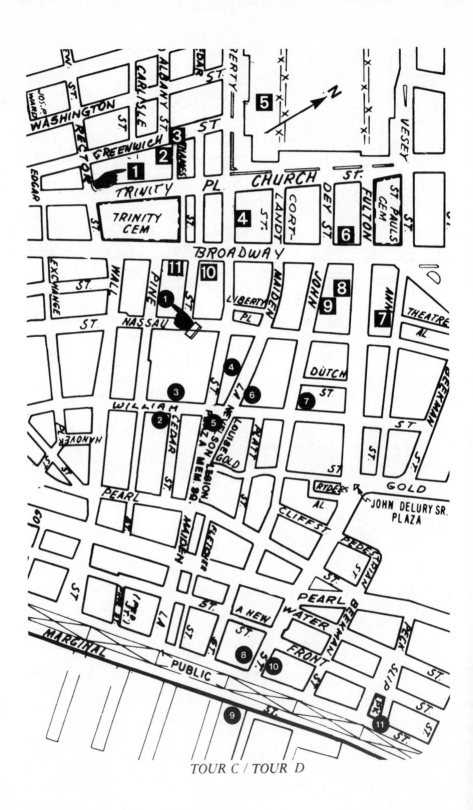

TOUR C / TOUR D

3
The Financial District

The American Beauty Rose can be produced in the splendor and fragrance which brings cheer to its beholder only by sacrificing the early buds which grow up around it. This is not an evil tendency in business. It is merely the working out of a law of nature and of God.

—John D. Rockefeller, Sr.

I spent 33 years, most of my time being a high-class muscle man for Big Business, for Wall Street and the bankers. In short, I was a racketeer for capitalism. I helped purify Nicaragua for the international banking house of Brown Brothers in 1909–1912. I helped make Mexico safe for American oil interests in 1914. I helped make Haiti and Cuba a decent place for the National City [Bank] boys to collect revenue in. I helped in the rape of half a dozen Central American republics for the benefit of Wall Street.

—Major General Smedley Butler,
United States Marines

In one sense, most of the southern half of Manhattan comprises the Financial District. But the central core of finance capital is the southern tip of the island. Here are the largest banks' main offices, the various exchanges (headed by the New York Stock Exchange), and many of the main offices of the country's largest insurance companies and corporate giants.

The history of New York began here. The Dutch, inaugurating their commercial exploitation of the New World's resources, "bought" the island from the Native Americans and lost it to the British. While the city gradually expanded northward, the area itself became a revolutionary hot spot in the 1770s, the center of mercantile capitalism in the first half of the nineteenth century, and the headquarters of finance and corporate capital after the Civil War. Rebuilding and re-rebuilding have gone on relentlessly, yet it is still possible to find traces of each epoch of the area's history.

Since the area is so compact, you may want to mix and match the tours. The Financial District is dotted with subway stations, which makes it possible to rearrange the routes.

TOUR A   *The Battery*

Subway information

Start and finish: Bowling Green
Station (IRT) #4 or #5 train

A1.   Battery Park* *(south of Bowling Green)*

Battery Park is a wide swath of green that covers the southern tip of Manhattan Island. At the entrance to the park you will see a flagpole commemorating the founding of New York in 1664 (a). On it is the Seal of New York, which amiably perpetuates the myth of European and Indian partnership. In fact, the Europeans got the land and the Native Americans gave the name Manhattan.

Battery Park is named for an early gun emplacement in a fort now known as Castle Clinton (b). This fortress is a relic of the postrevolutionary fear of the British. Its guns never fired at an enemy. It has been an opera house, an immigrants' depot, and an aquarium. Now it is only a shell, administered by the National Park Service.

Between 1855 and 1890 more than 8 million immigrants passed through this doorway, clutching their precious documents in one hand and their worldly possessions in the other. Many got their first job right off the boat. In a nineteenth-century version of the shapeup, employers would send agents to the port to sign up the exhausted and bewildered greenhorns before they had a chance to ask questions. Such was the paradox of this land of opportunity that many immigrants found themselves in a condition of virtual servitude while earning more money than they had ever seen before.

Shortly after Castle Clinton was replaced by Ellis Island as the port of entry, it became the New York City Aquarium. It quickly became the city's most popular attraction, drawing some 2.5 million visitors annually by the 1930s. Yet not ten years later it was gone, and therein lies a tale.

If there is one name that can be identified with the massive changes in the physiognomy of New York City in this century, it is that of Robert

---

*Sites inside Battery Park have been marked a, b, c, and d.

Courtesy of Michael Scurato/LNS

Moses, "the Master Builder." For five decades, Moses was appointed to post after important post by mayors and governors. At one time he held nearly a dozen commissionerships, coordinatorships, and chairmanships simultaneously. Over the years, he gained a reputation for arrogance, brilliance, vengefulness, and vindictiveness. In 1939 when he was head of the Triborough Bridge Authority, Moses decided to build a bridge to Brooklyn here at the Battery. He soon found himself locking horns with what he derisively called the "Goo-Goos"—"good government," old-money types who wanted to preserve the appearance of Lower Manhattan, and not incidentally, its land values.

When Moses was defeated and a tunnel built instead of his bridge (see Financial District A10), he took revenge by destroying the aquarium. In his capacity as parks commissioner, he ordered it closed "for the safety of the public." Behind locked fences, he demolished it. As a result of Moses' spite, the aquarium is now in a remote part of Brooklyn and all that remains of Castle Clinton is this dreary and sterile circle of stone.

On the water side of Castle Clinton, set in the ground near its southwest wall, is a memorial marker (c) to the Jewish poet Emma Lazarus (1849–1887). Her most famous work, "The New Colossus" (1886), is engraved on the base of the Statue of Liberty.* It is a passionate evocation of the image of this country as haven for the oppressed of the world.

*

"The New Colossus"

Not like the brazen giant of Greek fame,
With conquering limbs astride from land to land;
Here at our sea-washed, sunset gates shall stand
A mighty woman with a torch, whose flame
Is the imprisoned lightning, and her name
Mother of Exiles. From her beacon-hand
Glows world-wide welcome; her mild eyes command
The air-bridged harbor that twin cities frame.
"Keep, ancient lands, your storied pomp!" cries she
With silent lips. "Give me your tired, your poor,
Your huddled masses yearning to breathe free,
The wretched refuse of your teeming shore.
Send these, the homeless, tempest-tost to me,
I lift my lamp beside the golden door!"

Another view of the Great Lady is expressed in these lines by George Sterling (1869–1926):

"To the Goddess of Liberty"

Would One might pour within thy breast of bronze
Spirit and life! Then should thy loyal hand
Cast down its torch, and thy deep voice should cry:
"Turn back! Turn back, O liberative ships!
Be warned, ye voyagers! From tyranny
To vaster tyranny ye come! Ye come
From realms that in my morning twilight wait
My radiant invasion. But these shores
Have known and renounced me. I am raised
In mockery, and here the forfeit day
Deepens to West, and my indignant Star
Would hide her shame with darkness and the sea—
A sun of doom forecasting on the Land
The shadow of the sceptre and the sword."

Although it is not very prominent, don't overlook the monument dedicated to Admiral George Dewey (d). He was one of a long line of military "heroes" who have specialized in using U.S. firepower against third world peoples. In 1898–99 he completed the McKinley to Roosevelt to Dewey double play, which brought "the blessings of democracy" to Cuba and "our little brown brothers" in the Philippines.

In the park you can buy tickets for the ferries to Ellis Island and the Statue of Liberty. The ferries leave regularly throughout the day and the round-trip cost for each is $1.50 for adults and $.50 for children under 12. There is nothing now at Ellis Island except a hall filled with memories, but there is a Museum of Immigration inside the base of the Statue of Liberty. Although it has many moving and interesting pictures, the written commentary leans toward the melting-pot school of nostalgia with pronounced reverence for immigrants of the Andrew Carnegie stripe, those who "made it."

If you want a good view of the skyline and the Statue of Liberty for less money, take the Staten Island Ferry, which departs from just east of the park. A round trip costs only a quarter. The ferry has been in operation since 1712. One of its more illustrious pilots was Captain Cornelius Vanderbilt, who inflated his rank to "Commodore" when his fortune expanded. The name of the great man's first ferry was, if you can believe it, *The Mouse of the Mountain*!

As you leave the park you will pass a small playground—a nice place to rest even without children.

A2.   Jewish Memorial *(Whitehall and State Streets)*

At the base of a flagpole here is a memorial to "the 23 men, women and children who landed in September 1654 and founded the first Jewish Community in North America." Their ancestors had been booted out of Iberia the same year that Columbus "discovered" America. From there they went to Holland and thence to Brazil. When the Dutch ceded Brazil to the Portuguese, the Jews fled again. Their welcome in New Amsterdam was far from warm, and it wasn't until the authorities in old Amsterdam insisted that Peter Stuyvesant reluctantly agreed to put up with them—provided that they kept from becoming wards of the community.

A3.   Seaman's Church Institute *(State and Bridge Streets)*

Across the street from Battery Park is the Seaman's Church Institute, a lodging house and social service agency for merchant seamen. Its lobby looks and sounds like a working-class U.N. Its religious origins are perpetuated in the small chapel on the first floor. The public is invited to read the many informational plaques, among which is the heart-warming description of "crimping": a practice whereby sailors were decoyed into lodging houses and robbed. Sometimes whole crews were shanghaied onto ships in the same manner.

The circular staircase leading to the upper floors carries plaques in honor of the many benefactors of the institute. They read like a roster of the "400": Astor, Carnegie, Harriman, Morgan, Rockefeller, Schiff, Vanderbilt, etc., etc.

There are a reasonably priced cafeteria and a slightly more expensive restaurant in the building.

A4. **Former Army Induction Center*** *(Whitehall Street between Pearl and Water Streets)*

This huge red-brick building, with a carved panel in the doorway, fills the entire block. It looks as though it could last forever, but it is now abandoned and derelict. Arlo Guthrie immortalized the Army Induction

Army Medical Examiner: "At last a perfect soldier!"

Cartoon by Robert Minor

Center in "Alice's Restaurant": the place where you are "injected, inspected, detected, infected, neglected, and selected."

During the 1960s it was a favorite target for the antiwar movement. Draft-card burnings, mass arrests, and guerrilla theater were almost daily occurrences. In December 1965, 61 people were arrested while they picketed and sang Christmas carols; two years later 3,000 demonstrated and 261 were arrested. The Army Induction Center came to stand for all that was despicable about the Vietnam War.

A5.   **Fraunces Tavern** *(54 Pearl Street, near Broad Street)*
This building is a reconstruction of the inn where George Washington delivered his famous farewell to his officers at the end of the Revolutionary War. Sam Fraunces, owner of the inn and later steward to Washington, was a Black man, a fact deftly concealed by most literature on the tavern. The brochure produced by the Sons of the Revolution, those worthy brothers of the DAR, who administer the building, call him "a man of French extraction from the West Indies." The tavern is presently both a historical monument and a working restaurant.

On January 24, 1975, the building next door was bombed by the FALN, a Puerto Rican nationalist group, in retaliation for the killing of two Puerto Rican revolutionaries in a restaurant in Puerto Rico two weeks before. The bombing shocked the city and produced mixed reactions on the Left. The Puerto Rican Socialist Party, for instance, condemned the bombing.

A6.   **Coenties Slip**
In the early days of the city, this was a quiet residential neighborhood. Something of its character is conveyed in this small newspaper advertisement:

> Isaac Brinckerhoff, No. 8 Coenties Slip, has for sale, a likely Negro wench, aged 33 years, with her female child, also a smart Negro boy, 12 years of age.*

The selling of parent and child together was an attempt to circumvent a law passed in 1758, which mandated freedom for the children of slaves. Such were the concerns of those who trafficked in human beings.

A7.   **Broad and South William Streets**
In 1740 there were 10,000 citizens and 2,000 slaves in New York City, and fear of the slaves was rampant. A rumor that they were poisoning the water

---

*Frederick Collins, *Money Town* (New York: Putnam, 1946).

supply caused most citizens to drink bottled water for months. In the spring of the following year, a rash of suspicious fires erupted in private residences and official buildings, including the governor's house, the King's Chapel, and the army barracks.

At this intersection stood the home of one Robert Hogg. When this prominent citizen's house went up in flames, many felt certain that a slave revolt was imminent. En masse, they left town so that the militia could deal with the supposed uprising. Some 150 Blacks and 25 whites were arrested. Thirty-one Blacks and four whites were executed and 70 slaves were banished to the West Indies.

The existence of slavery was a perpetual source of anxiety to the body politic. Despite legal attempts to restrict the movement of slaves, rumors of revolts persisted, in some cases with justification (see Financial District B3, for instance).

Presently at this location is the International Telephone and Telegraph Building. They too are highly security conscious: visitors are exhorted in four places to "report to the Security Office before proceeding" anywhere else. In the Security Office sits the security officer, scanning and tracking on six television screens.

Over the door on the southeast corner is a mosaic in which mythology, religion, and electrocommunication are tied into one big, tangled knot: a winged and haloed angel links the hemispheres with a bolt of lightning. Thus does Mammon flatter itself.

A8.   Beaver and Broad Streets

By June 1775 everyone knew that an attempt at independence was in the offing. When the British military tried to evacuate the city surreptitiously, they were met at this intersection by the Sons of Liberty, led by Marinus Willett. (See Lower East Side A9.) The militants relieved the British of their weapons and then wished them Godspeed. A year later, the guns were in the hands of the first group of New York volunteers.

A9.   Standard Oil Building *(26 Broadway, near Beaver Street)*

Before the antitrust laws cloned Standard Oil in 1911, this was its royal counting house and stands as an example of the public corporate image of its time. Until the World War II blackout, a perpetual oil flame burned atop its tower, and could be seen for miles around. Inside the lobby the logo "S O" appears everywhere in ironwork and in metal filigree. High on the walls the names of the original board of directors stare down at us. Below the name John D. Rockefeller stands an empty pedestal. The old man was carted off by grandson Nelson when the building was sold in 1956. Facing the Broadway entrance is a gilded clock. Before the salt air damaged it, the entire ceiling was gilded.

In 1913 the Rockefeller-owned mines around Ludlow, Colorado, were struck. Ludlow was a company town and, when the strikers were locked out, they were forced to spend the entire winter in tents. The following spring, management escalated the struggle. The National Guard and hired thugs charged into the tent colony, shooting their guns and setting fire to the tents. More than 30 people died in what became known as the Ludlow Massacre. The coast-to-coast headlines horrified the whole country. Upton Sinclair, Socialist and author, organized a "mourning picket line" in front of this building: a line of marchers wearing black crepe. As one might expect, they were arrested for daring to challenge the mighty Rockefeller empire.

A10.   **Brooklyn-Battery Tunnel Entrance** *(between Greenwich Street and WUI Plaza)*

As you stand on the overpass, looking into the tunnel, you may want to think of the 150 families who received two weeks' eviction notice from Robert Moses in 1940, when construction began. Fifteen years later, when the tunnel was completed, 338 long black limousines brought the dignitaries to the opening ceremonies. None of the evictees had been invited.

A11.   **Bowling Green Park** *(Broadway and Battery Place)*

Bowling Green Park is a small triangle of green set off by the massive bulk of the U.S. Custom House. During the colonial period it was fenced in and leased to the local gentry for the fee of one peppercorn per year. When the British imposed the onerous Stamp Act on the colonies, rioting broke out here. The British responded by erecting a statue of George III.

Neither statue nor fence could prevent the inevitable: on July 9, 1776, following the first public reading of the Declaration of Independence (see Financial District B9), King George was toppled for conversion into bullets. (Revolutionaries have always been poets!) The event is illustrated on the Heritage Marker in the park.

In 1788 there was a huge parade down Broadway to Bowling Green in support of the ratification of the Constitution. The artisans in the parade marched by craft, in distinctive dress, and there were floats symbolizing the various crafts. It must have been quite a sight to see butchers, bakers, hatmakers, pewterers, coopers, blacksmiths, and printers in colorful attire, demonstrating for the new Constitution!

The Custom House stands solidly at the edge of the park, a monument to the power of the mercantile class. The statues along the roof each represents one of the great mercantile nations of the world.

TOUR B   Wall Street

Subway information

Start: Wall Street Station (IRT) #2
or #3 train
Finish: Rector Street Station (BMT)
N or RR train, or Wall Street
Station (IRT) #4 or #5 train

B1.   Hanover Square

New York City's first printing press was set up by William Bradford in a building in Hanover Square in 1693. The area subsequently became known as "printing house square." Bradford came from Philadelphia, where he had been tried for printing allegedly seditious material. Although found innocent, he thought it politic to move here, eventually establishing New York's first newspaper, the *Gazette*, in 1725. By then he had become a Tory. In 1735, faced with John Peter Zenger's upstart competition, the *Journal*, Bradford found himself attacking the same principles that had provided the basis for his own defense (see Financial District B9).

Named in honor of the British House of Hanover, the square was one of the few places to escape the orgy of name-changing after the Revolution. When the printers moved uptown, Hanover Square became the city's main commercial center. It is now a pleasant place to sit and rest while touring. The statue in the square is of Abraham de Peyster, one of New York's earliest mayors.

B2.   7 Hanover Sq. *(on Water Street near Old Slip)*

In 1850 this site was occupied by the firm of Tilton & Mahoney. One of its employees was a Black man, James Hamlet, who was the first person to be seized under the provisions of the Fugitive Slave Law. Since the law prohibited accused fugitives from testifying on their own behalf, Hamlet could not explain that in fact he was a free Negro, not a fugitive slave. (For the story of his "ransom," see Civic Center/Lower West Side C3.) Within 15 years of this incident, there were no fugitive slaves; there were only ex-slaves.

B3.   Wall Street *(and South Street)*

We now arrive at Wall Street, which has come to stand in the eyes of the world for American Imperialism. The Dutch, after several unpleasant incidents, became wary of the Native Americans (who, likewise, were learning to be suspicious of the Dutch). So they built a wall to keep them out.

In 1711 a slave market was set up at the foot of Wall Street. Both

Blacks and Native Americans were bought, sold, and hired. (The latter refers to the neat trick of a slaveowner renting out his slaves to less wealthy citizens who needed their labor power.)

The first slave revolt in the city occurred on April 6, 1712 (see Financial District D6). A group of 30 Blacks set fire to the building of a slaveowner. When the citizenry tried to put out the fire, the slaves descended upon them with guns, knives, and hatchets, killing nine and wounding six. They fled to the woods nearby, where they were hunted down and executed in a most barbarous manner. Of the three leaders, one was burnt alive, one was broken on the wheel, and the third was left hanging on a chain to die slowly.

At the foot of Wall Street stood Murray's Wharf. Here, on April 22, 1774, militants staged "the New York Tea Party," modeled after the Boston soirée. However, they were bolder than the Bostonians, scorning disguises while despatching the cargo.

During the Revolution, when New York was occupied by the British, Wall Street was the most elegant and fashionable place in the city, where the leading Tories paraded in their finery (see Financial District B13). But when the war was over in 1783, 'twas the rebels' turn. When General Washington landed at Murray's Wharf he was met by crowds throwing flowers. Most of the Tories had been stripped of their property and had departed with the British.

B4.   100 Wall Street *(at Water Street)*
Inside the door of this building, on the right-hand side, is another of those classy historical plaques that can be seen throughout the city, presenting a laundered view of our history. These plaques tend to focus on the Great White Settler and delicately omit all reference to Native Americans or slaves.

B5.   Wall and Water Streets
Here, on the southeast corner, stood the Merchant's Coffee House, one of the several "publick houses" that were meeting places for revolutionary plotters in the 1770s. Next to it, and still in existence, is the Tontine Coffee House, where the stock exchange agreement was formalized (see Financial District B11). *Tontines* were early cooperative mutual insurance clubs for merchants, the forerunners of today's multimillion-dollar insurance industry.

Also at this site stood a marble statue of William Pitt, the British statesman. He became a hero to the Americans for opposing the Stamp Act and other onerous taxes. When the Declaration of Independence was signed and the statue of George III toppled from its pedestal in Bowling

Green, British soldiers retaliated by knocking off the head and arms of the statue of Pitt (see Lower East Side A8).

B6.   60 Wall Street

Here lived Captain Kidd in the last decade of the seventeenth century, before he came to a bad end on a London gallows. Most of the pirates who subsequently had their offices hereabouts died comfortably in bed.

B7.   The Bank of New York *(48 Wall Street, at William Street)*

This bank, the first in the city, was founded by Alexander Hamilton. On the ground floor is a plaque describing its establishment during a meeting at the Merchant's Coffee House nearby. Hamilton's enmity with Aaron Burr, which ended in their duel and Hamilton's death, was fueled by Burr's opening the Bank of Manhattan.

B8.   40 Wall Street

Before its merger with Chase, this was the site of the main branch of the Bank of Manhattan, which had broken the monopoly of Hamilton's Bank of New York. It owes its existence to a typical piece of early capitalist chicanery. The Manhattan Company was chartered as a water company to provide that essential liquid to a growing city. But Aaron Burr's real desire was to break into finance capital. Through political influence in Albany, the state capital, Burr and his syndicate arranged for the following obscure clause to be included in his water company's charter:

> The surplus capital of the company may be employed in any way not inconsistent with the laws and Constitution of the United States or the State of New York.

After going through the motions of digging a well and laying some pipe near Spring Street (see Civic Center/Lower West Side D1), Burr built his bank while the water company languished and died.

B9.   Wall and Nassau Streets

On November 2, 1734, by order of Governor Cosby's Provincial Council, John Peter Zenger's newspaper, the *New-York Weekly Journal*, was publicly burned at this spot. In a recent election, Zenger had supported the Popular Party in opposition to William Bradford's Tory *Gazette*. When a bricklayer, a painter, and a baker, along with other artisans, took their seats at the council, Zenger printed some anonymous songs

> To you good lads that dare oppose
> All lawless power and might,
> You are the theme that we have chose
> And to your praise we write. . . .

Whereupon Cosby, in a fit of pique, had the *Journal* burned and its publisher jailed.

While in jail, Zenger was held incommunicado. The pressure brought to bear by his infuriated readers resulted in his release from solitary confinement. Zenger was then able to dictate articles to his wife through a hole in the prison door and she put out the paper.

Even before the trial began, Cosby tried to sabotage the defense by summarily disbarring Zenger's obstreperous attornies. When the next, court-appointed lawyer seemed none too strong, Cosby appeared to have won the battle. Then, in the midst of the trial, Andrew Hamilton, the old and respected lawyer from Philadelphia, stepped forward and volunteered his services; Cosby lost the war.

Hamilton's defense was based upon the assertion that Zenger had been printing the truth and that therefore his words could not have been libelous. Zenger's acquittal established freedom of the press as a legal right; the term "Philadelphia lawyer" became synonymous with legal acuity.

In 1765 this spot was the site of the Stamp Act Congress. This gathering of delegates from nine colonies was the first step along the path that led to the Continental Congress and the drafting of the Declaration of Independence. These assemblies, as they gathered increasing public support from the colonists, eventually became an alternative government to that of the British colonial administration.

Ten years after the Stamp Act Congress, there was a British arsenal here. When news reached New York of the events at Lexington and Concord, radicals broke into the arsenal and seized some 600 muskets, which were subsequently put to good use.

Federal Hall, which stands here now, was built in 1842. It is a national monument, housing a museum of colonial and Revolutionary War history. Admission is free and the building is open during business hours Monday through Friday.

B10.   Morgan Guaranty Trust Company *(23 Wall Street)*

This is the headquarters of the Morgan financial empire. In 1908, during a stock market panic, J. P. called a meeting in his offices here of the heads of the major Wall Street banks and warned them that the Stock Exchange would go under unless they acted quickly. In five minutes he raised $27 million. (That's what financial emperors are for.)

On September 16, 1920, a wagonload of explosives blew up in front of the building, killing 33 and injuring 400. "Anarchists" were blamed for the explosion (that's what anarchists are for), but no individual was ever charged. The scars of the explosion may still be seen on the building.

One would never suspect that under this austere edifice lies a warm heart. In the 1820s the site was occupied by Downing's Oyster House, which had an underground railroad station in its basement. (The underground railroad had no trains or tracks. Its passengers were escaped slaves and its conductors were Abolitionists. It operated at night, its route was south to north, and its last stop was freedom.)

B11. **The New York Stock Exchange** *(Wall and Broad Streets)*
The Stock Exchange was founded in 1792 by a group of brokers, who met under a buttonwood (sycamore) tree and agreed on this friendly price-fixing deal:

> We the subscribers, brokers for the purchase and sale of public stock, do hereby solemnly promise and pledge ourselves that we will not buy or sell from this day, from any person whatsoever, any kind of public stock at a less rate than one-quarter per cent commission on the special value, and that we will give a preference to each other in our negotiations.*

Visitors are treated to a tedious display that instructs us on the virtue of "people's capitalism," while congratulating us on the power of the great corporations. Hours are 10 A.M. to 4 P.M. on business days–naturally. Admission is free, unlike a seat on the Exchange.

As we near the nerve center of the Exchange, the tone darkens: "No cameras allowed. Visitors' gallery partitioned from trading floor by bulletproof 1 1/16-inch thick glass." Here is the story behind these extraordinary precautions. The visitors' gallery was always an open balcony overlooking the floor of the Exchange. In 1966 a group from Youth Against War and Fascism made use of this easy access and bombarded the brokers with leaflets condemning the Vietnam War and its corporate supporters. A year later the Yippies floated dollar bills over the balcony, causing a mad scramble on the floor that thoroughly disrupted trade. Unnerved by the prospect of further attacks on its dignity and steadfastness, the Stock Exchange sealed itself off.

Outside the Exchange things have not always been all business. On April 5, 1971, the Southern Christian Leadership Conference Poor People's Mule Train came to Wall Street. More than 3,000 people filled this narrow street, roaring their approval, as George Wiley said, "If we have to tear down the buildings on Wall Street brick by brick, if we have to go into the Chase Manhattan Bank, then I say Power to the People!"

B12. **1 Wall Street** *(at Broadway)*
In front of the building is a plaque explaining the origin of the name of the street. It is notable for its omission of the fact that the wall was erected to

---

*Frederick Collins, *Moneytown*.

keep Native Americans out and in neglecting to mention that the wall fell into disrepair because the locals disrepaired it by removing large sections for firewood.

B13.   **Trinity Church** *(Broadway and Wall Street)*
The dark, elegant facade of this church conceals many stories. In 1693, when Anglicanism became New York's official religion, the king chartered Trinity Church to administer the parish of New York. All citizens, regardless of their religion (or whether they were indeed believers), were taxed to build the church and pay its rector. In 1705 Queen Anne granted Trinity an enormous piece of land, including most of the territory between Broadway and the Hudson River, from Fulton Street to well above what is now Spring Street. This became known as the Trinity Grab, and for more than a century descendants of those whose land had been confiscated sued the church unsuccessfully. Trinity's holdings generated enormous wealth in rents, augmented by such additional royal perks as the right to seize any hapless whale or unclaimed shipwreck that landed on its shores.

During the Revolution, Trinity was a nest of Tories. While the city was occupied by the British, gentlemen and officers enjoyed strolling with their ladies on Wall Street and on Broadway past the church. After the Revolution, many of its parishioners and some of its clergy fled the country. In the Chapel of All Saints, to the right of the altar, is a plaque in memory of Charles Inglis, a Tory rector who departed for Nova Scotia in 1783.

As a landlord, Trinity has acted with a singular lack of Christian charity. In 1857 the public learned that Trinity was holding $600,000 worth of mortgages on smaller churches, foreclosing without mercy when they were unable to make payments. When a Black parish asked for a $100 donation, Trinity refused. Two generations later Trinity was exposed in public hearings as a slumlord. The rents it charged were so high that tenants were compelled to take in boarders. As the *Weekly People*, the Socialist Labor Party paper, noted:

> A witness stated that she found in 1893, 139 families had 214 boarders. Sometimes two families occupied one apartment. The overcrowding she found mostly in East 11th Street, Mulberry, Mott and especially Elizabeth Streets. Most families live in an apartment of two rooms, dark and unhealthy. . . .

Even its churchyard has a hidden history. In the early 1700s a law was passed that read, "No Negro shall be buried in Trinity Churchyard." Among those who did make it to the hallowed grounds were Alexander Hamilton and William Bradford. In the northeast corner of the churchyard stands a monument to the Revolutionary soldiers, acknowledging finally their achievement of legitimacy.

The present church is the third on the site. In 1776 the Revolutionists evacuated the city, taking with them all the church bells to convert into cannon. Since these bells were the fire alarm system of the time, when a fire broke out there was no way of summoning the bucket brigade. In the ensuing conflagration, much of the city was destroyed, including the original Trinity Church. The second church was also destroyed by fire.

When this building was dedicated on May 21, 1846, its steeple was the highest structure in the New York skyline, dominating the heavens as it did the earth. After the dedication ceremony, the curious were charged an admission fee to climb the 308 steps to the top of the spire to look out over the surrounding countryside. The church and graveyard are open from 7 A.M. to 6 P.M. daily; the exhibit room is open Monday to Friday from 10:30 A.M. to 4 P.M.

TOUR C   *The Twin Towers, Ma Bell, and Company*

Subway information

Start: Rector Street Station (BMT)
N or RR train
Finish: Wall Street Station (IRT) #4
or #5 train

C1.   **The American Stock Exchange** *(86 Trinity Place)*
Before it found a home at this address, the "little brother" to the much larger New York Stock Exchange was called the Curb Exchange, because that was where trading was done.

C2.   **Albany and Greenwich Streets**
In the first half of the nineteenth century the Planters' Hotel occupied this site. It was so named for the southern planters who patronized it. Its location was convenient to the Perth Amboy Ferry, which connected with the southern rail lines. The hotel closed for lack of clients when the Civil War broke out.

Albany Street ends here, in spite of the efforts of progressive city planners. Although the extension of the street won municipal approval four separate times, Trinity Church, whose churchyard would have been bisected, succeeded in blocking the plan. Other graveyards didn't fare so well (see Greenwich Village A12).

C3.   Greenwich and Thames Streets

In the 1740s there was a tavern here that was a meeting place for slaves. Mary Burton, an indentured servant who worked at the tavern, turned informer, which led to the arrest of 175 people and many executions and deportations (see Financial District A7).

C4.   The United States Steel Building *(1 Liberty Plaza)*

A perfect example of Marshall McLuhan's observation that "the medium is the message," the U.S. Steel Building clothes itself in exposed structural steel. Hard, cold, massive, and black, it is a metaphor of industrialism at its most enormous and impersonal.

On the ground floor are the offices of Merrill, Lynch, Pierce, Fenner, & Smith, the stockbrokers who call themselves "a breed apart." Here you can gaze in dazed amazement as the Money Tree shows you the "Distribution of Funds in the United States," and computerized, electronic figures keep rising at alarming, incomprehensible rates. Or you may stand with the old pensioners and young execs on their lunch hours watching the stock quotations fly by. Or try your hand at a personal Telequote machine, which stands like a one-armed bandit, ready to inform you of the state of your fortune, if you have one.

On the seamier side, the firm was recently hit with a lawsuit charging it with racism and sexism. It was obliged to pay to its employees $3.5 million in restitution, thus demonstrating the power of the workers against Merrill Lynch's bull.

C5.   The World Trade Center

This is New York's latest entry in the Anything-You-Can-Do-We-Can-Do-Bigger sweeps. Each tower stands 110 stories high. For three bucks (half-price for kids) you can take the two-floors-per-second elevator to the top of the South Tower and look down on the anonymous masses below. The view is staggering. Or buy a drink at the Windows on the World restaurant at the top of the North Tower, where you can look as long as you like. (Don't order food, though; the prices are as high as the towers.)

The World Trade Center was another piece of the Rockefellers' design to revivify the Financial District, begun two years after Chase Manhattan Plaza (see Financial District D3). It was subsidized by public Port Authority bonds and further bolstered by Governor Nelson Rockefeller's promise to house state offices there. Now that office space is at a premium, the state offices are moving again. (First place in the Excessively Large Building Contest is now held by the Sears Tower in Chicago.)

In the middle of what is now the World Trade Center, where Washington Street used to lie between Dey and Cortlandt Streets, there stood in 1837 the firm of Eli Hart & Company. The winter of 1836 was especially severe and, to make matters worse, there was a scarcity of flour—and what flour was available was very high priced. Convinced that merchants were holding out for still higher prices, a crowd of four or five thousand gathered in front of City Hall on the night of February 10, 1837. They marched to Hart's warehouse, broke in, and destroyed hundreds of barrels of grain and flour. The riot was quelled by the police and the militia.

C6. The American Telephone and Telegraph Building *(Broadway between Fulton and Dey Streets)*

The former headquarters of this giant corporation stands as a monument to pomposity. It boasts more marble than any other office building in the city, and more columns than any other building in the world, including the Parthenon. From the outside you will see the columns marching up the building, floor by floor. But you must go inside to savor the grandiosity of the lobby, where a forest of columns supported the largest monopoly in the world.*

Dey Street, the short block leading from Broadway to the World Trade Center, was notorious as a site of auctions of indentured servants in the eighteenth century.

C7. 22 Ann Street *(south of Theater Alley)*

Here Horace Greeley edited a weekly newspaper, the *New Yorker*. His reaction to the Panic of 1837 was to write:

> Mechanics and Artisans, laborers, you cannot with safety give heed to those who prophecy smooth things.... We say to the unemployed, you who are able to leave the cities should do so without delay.... Fly—scatter through the land—go to the Great West.

which has become known as "go west, young man." Greeley was rather a leftist who, when he edited the *Tribune*, employed Karl Marx as a correspondent. (See also Civic Center/Lower West Side A11.)

Down Ann Street, at Broadway, stood Hampden Hall, the headquarters of the Sons of Liberty after they moved from Montagne's Tavern (see Civic Center/Lower West Side A8).

At the other end of Theater Alley, the Park Theater was erected in 1795. In 1808 a new owner inaugurated the policy of importing a single leading player for each new production. This money-making innovation

---

*Having recently determined that the exact center of the universe is located in midtown Manhattan, AT & T has moved its headquarters to a new building on Madison Avenue.

soon led to the tyranny of the star system and the death of theater companies. The star system parallels the rise of individualism in the socioeconomic system; it is the theatrical equivalent of early competitive capitalism.

In January 1829 one of those stars, a radical named Fanny Wright, delivered a "Highly successful series of lectures here," according to the Owenite *Free Enquirer* (see Lower East Side B6). Wright was a millionaire utopian socialist who worked to eliminate slavery, demanded women's rights, fought for workers' rights, and agitated for birth control. In addition to all this, she was a playwright who wrote one play on the Swiss struggle for independence and another, set in ancient Athens, which develops her materialist philosophy.

C8.   Fulton Street *(east of Broadway)*

Just before the Civil War, the Communist Club of New York was founded at 148 Fulton Street. It was led by Joseph Wedemeyer, a German emigré and a friend and correspondent of Marx and Engels. The building and even the number 148 have long since vanished.

At 150 Fulton Street is a moderately priced health food restaurant called Nature's Kitchen, which serves well-prepared food in large portions.

C9.   11 John Street *(near Broadway)*

This skinny old building houses a number of progressive organizations: the National Federation of Independent Unions, the New York City Unemployed and Welfare Council, and the Women's Committee for Unionization. The NFIU is aiming to organize that section of the population that has been ignored by the traditional labor movement: domestic workers, tenants, public service workers, and so forth. The Unemployed and Welfare Council does everything from publicizing welfare rights to supplying emergency benefits and services. The WCU hopes to organize all working women. It sponsors training sessions and puts out a monthly newsletter.

C10.   Marine Midland Grace Trust Company *(140 Broadway)*

On August 20, 1969, this building was bombed by urban guerrillas. The perpetrators sent a letter to the underground newspaper, *Rat*:

> The explosive device set off at the Marine Midland grace [sic] Trust Company on the night of August 20th was an act of political sabotage. . . .
> Crimes against other peoples of the world are every bit as heinous as crimes against Americans. Jailing and killing will not deter acts of sabotage in the U.S.; nor will the age-old political placebo known as

> "liberal reform." Nor will the longed for ending of the war in Vietnam even begin to end the war in the U.S. Nor in short is there anything the government can do to placate the impulse to revolution that is in the blood of young America from coast to coast.

Despite a raid on *Rat*'s office, the police were never able to find the letter.

No, the cube on its point was not upended by the bombing. It was designed to be that way by its sculptor, Isamu Noguchi.

Across the street, where there is now a park, were the offices of the IRT. (For more information on the IRT, see Civic Center/Lower West Side A1.) During a Transport Workers Union organizing drive in the mid-1930s, lunch-hour demonstrations were staged here daily. After being served enough of these lunchtime treats, the IRT succumbed and recognized the union.

C11.   The Equitable Building *(120 Broadway)*

Thames Street, between Trinity Place and Broadway, is one of the darkest streets in Manhattan. A major reason for the gloom is the looming mass of the Equitable Building.

This beehive of offices was built in 1915, exploiting the land—as well as the light and air above it—in a more gluttonous fashion than any building had done previously. There was such an outcry from its neighbors that the following year the city was forced to create its first zoning laws. These provided for a maximum ratio of building mass to land area of 12:1, as compared with Equitable's ratio of 30:1.

The building is flanked by Pine and Cedar Streets. Before the Revolution they were King Street and Little Queen Street, respectively. In 1794 the names were changed for obvious reasons.

TOUR D   *Gold Vaults and Fish Stalls*

Subway information

Start: Wall Street Station (IRT) #2
or #3 train
Finish: Fulton Street Station (IRT)
#2 or #3 train

D1.   The Downtown Club *(60 Pine Street)*

If you are walking around the Financial District at lunchtime, you may wonder where the bigshots eat. Rest assured, the men who manage the money don't mix with the masses at McDonald's. Clubs such as this serve gourmet lunches in opulent surroundings to members only. And if the trip to the club seems too tiresome or the negotiations too delicate, many large firms have their own dining rooms, where executives and their clients can wheel, deal, and dine in luxury and privacy—a little bonus they give themselves at the expense of the stockholders.

D2.   Off-Track Betting Parlor *(Cedar and William Streets)*
The OTB is a device to help the State raise money, mostly from the pockets of the poor, who yearn to make a quick killing. But the OTB parlor here is different. Unlike the seedy establishments uptown, this one has a sign in burnished iron over an elegant corner entrance.

D3.   Chase Manhattan Plaza
Here stands the Rockefeller House of Money, completed in 1960. The fifth basement vault alone is the size of a football field and is said to hold almost $50 billion in securities and more than $4 million in cash. Its construction

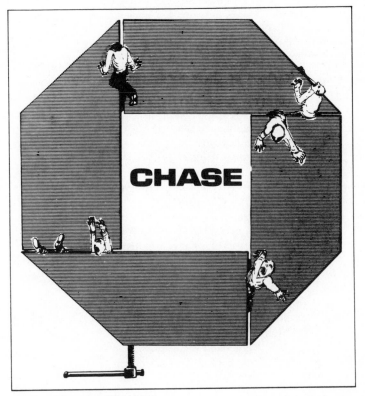

Courtesy of Gregg Willard/LNS

was the Rockefeller family's grand gesture to revivify the Financial District.

The growth of the giant that is Chase Manhattan was accomplished through a series of mergers somewhat akin to the biblical *begats*, except that they were more like *betakes*. Here is a partial list of the appetite of the omnivorous Chase, through 1931, before it merged with the Bank of Manhattan (each bank is shown with the banks it had previously swallowed):*

    I. Metropolitan Bank: 1921
        a. Maiden Lane National Bank: 1905
        b. National Shoe & Leather Bank: 1906
        c. Hamilton Trust Company: 1921
    II. Mechanics and Metals National Bank: 1926
        a. Leather Manufacturers National Bank: 1904
        b. National Copper Bank: 1910
        c. Fourth National Bank: 1914
        d. New York Produce Exchange Bank: 1920
        e. Lincoln Trust Company: 1922
    III. Mutual Bank: 1927
    IV. Garfield National Bank: 1929
    V. National Park Bank: 1929
        a. Wells Fargo & Company Bank: 1911
    VI. Interstate Trust Company: 1930
        a. Franklin National Bank: 1927
        b. Bloomingdale Brothers, Private Bankers: 1927
        c. Hamilton National Bank: 1928
        d. Century Bank: 1929
            1. Dewey State Bank: 1928
    VII. Equitable Trust Company: 1930
        a. Bowling Green Trust Company: 1909
        b. Madison Trust Company: 1911
        c. Trust Company of America: 1912
            1. North American Trust Company: 1905
                a. International Bankers & Trust Company: 1900
            2. City Trust Company: 1905
            3. Trust Company of North America: 1905
            4. Colonial Trust Company: 1907
        d. Importers & Traders National Bank: 1923
        e. Seaboard National Bank: 1929
            1. Mercantile Trust Company: 1922
            2. New Netherland Bank: 1928
    VIII. American Express Bank & Trust Company: 1931

---

*Frank L. Walton, *Tomahawks to Textiles* (New York City: Appleton, Century, Crofts, 1953).

In December 1965 a large rally was held in Chase Manhattan Plaza. A. Philip Randolph, head of a Committee of Conscience Against Apartheid, urged the withdrawal of accounts from Chase in protest of its involvement in the South African economy. Almost 20 years later the Chase connection with South Africa is as strong as ever.

At Liberty and Nassau Streets, right in the middle of what is now Chase Plaza, there stood during the Revolution the Livingston Sugar House, which the British converted into a prison. Between 1776 and 1783 captured Revolutionary soldiers and political prisoners were incarcerated here under the most horrendous conditions imaginable. Local citizens risked their own safety to smuggle food inside; nevertheless, many prisoners died of starvation or cold.

D4.   Federal Reserve Bank *(33 Liberty Street)*

This is the "bank for banks," a stone fortress in the style of the Italian Renaissance of the Medicis and the Borgias. Here, the gold holdings of nations are moved from room to room according to the fluctuations of trade. In vaults that descend five levels below the street, there is more gold than any other place in the United States, including Fort Knox.

There are free tours by appointment, Monday through Friday on the hour from 10 A.M. through 2 P.M. Call 791-6130.

Liberty Street was originally named Crown Street. Its name was one of those changed in 1794.

D5.   Louise Nevelson Plaza *(Maiden Lane, William and Liberty Streets)*

This small triangle has been dedicated recently to one of the country's leading sculptors. It contains five of her enormous cast iron pieces, set in a pleasant park.

D6.   The Home Insurance Building *(59 Maiden Lane)*

On the fifteenth floor of this building is the Harold V. Smith Firefighting Museum, owned by the Home Insurance Company. The link between firefighting and insurance may seem obscure until you realize that putting out fires saves property—originally the sole interest of insurance companies. The museum has a large collection of firemarks, those small, metal medallions bearing the insurer's name, which told the firemen that the building was covered. In an early version of the protection racket, firemen would extinguish fires only in insured buildings.

The curator of the collection is knowledgeable and enthusiastic: she will feed you all sorts of information if you show interest. The museum is open Monday through Friday from 10 A.M. to 3:30 P.M. and it is free. Outside the building is a plaque marking the site of Thomas Jefferson's residence.

Maiden Lane was so named because it overlooked a brook where young women took the family wash in the olden days. (Since they were unmarried, they were ipso facto "maidens" in those unliberated days.) Immediately north of Maiden Lane was a meadow. It was here, in April 1712, that a conspiracy of slaves led to the city's first major slave rebellion (see Financial District B3).

"The Crocker National Bank board of directors meeting stands adjourned. The Metropolitan Life Insurance Company's board of directors will please come to order."

Conrad/LNS

D7. William Street *(at John Street)*

On the northwest corner of this intersection is a plaque commemorating the Battle of Golden Hill, which took place in January 1770. Provoked by the destruction of the fourth Liberty Pole (see Civic Center/Lower West Side A7), the citizens resolved to treat as enemies all armed British soldiers found in the streets after roll call. The soldiers responded by posting handbills characterizing the patriots as "traitors." When two colonists tried to stop the soldiers from putting up the posters, a skirmish began, which soon escalated into a full-fledged battle. The first blood of the Revolution had been shed.

William Street now ends only a few blocks uptown, at Beekman Street. At one time there were several important addresses on the part of the street now occupied by Beekman Hospital and Pace University. In 1786 the African Free School was founded at 245 William Street. This was the first school for Blacks in New York.

A century later, the Socialist Labor Party was housed at 184 William

Street. The SLP was the first Marxist party in the United States. Founded in 1876, the year of the dissolution of the First International (see Lower East Side B6), it soon came under the charismatic dominance of Daniel De Leon. In 1900 the SLP split, largely over the issue of De Leon's rigid approach to leadership and to socialism. Out of the split grew the Socialist Party. The SLP remained a force, although diminished in influence, until De Leon's death in 1914. It continues to exist today, publishing pamphlets and its newspaper, the *People*.

(The next four entries are somewhat out of the way, but we believe they are worth the extra walk.)

D8.   **Sweets Restaurant** *(Fulton Street, near South Street)*
This seafood restaurant proclaims proudly that it was established in 1845. What it fails to mention was that its patrons were "blackbirders": middlemen who trafficked in slaves long after slavery had been outlawed in New York and even after the slave trade had been banned nationwide. These smugglers of human beings moved their "cargo" from arriving ships onto railroad cars for transportation south.

Edward Sweet, the owner of the restaurant at the time, was killed in the Wall Street explosion of 1920 (see Financial District B10).

D9.   **South Street Seaport Museum** *(South Street, near Fulton Street)*
This unusual museum is interesting for its glimpse of maritime life during the height of nineteenth-century mercantile capitalism. On two piers at the foot of Fulton Street and several blocks west of these piers are restored ships, marine art galleries, bookstores, and shops housed in carefully restored buildings. In the summer excellent concerts are held outdoors on the end of the dock. There is a charge to board the ships, but you may wander along the piers and into the shops and exhibits for free.

D10.   **Fulton Fish Market** *(South Street, between Beekman Street and Slip)*
At one time this was the largest wholesale fish market on the Atlantic coast. It was established in 1821 "to supply the common people with the necessities of life at a reasonable price." Activity was at a peak in the early hours of the morning. By noon, the market was deserted.

D11.   **Peck Slip** *(near South Street)*
In olden times there was a ferry to Brooklyn that departed from here. (Actually it was only a rowboat, but that was adequate for seventeenth-century traffic.) Imagining this bucolic scene may bring mist to the eyes of the nostalgic. Native Americans looked upon it with different eyes: they were charged double fare.

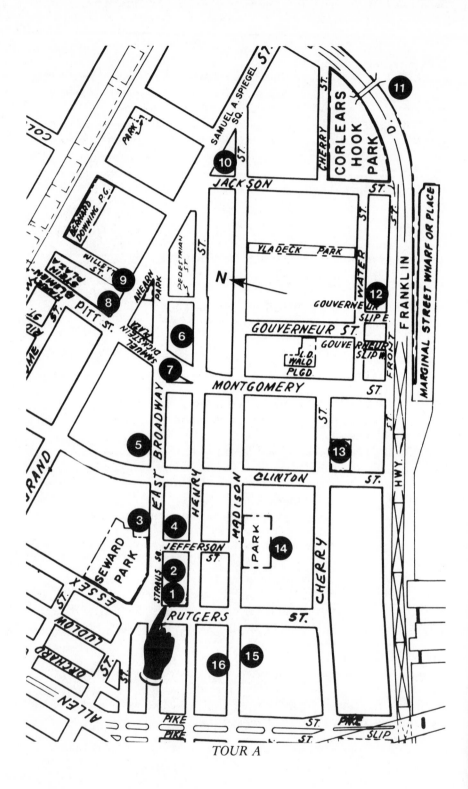

TOUR A

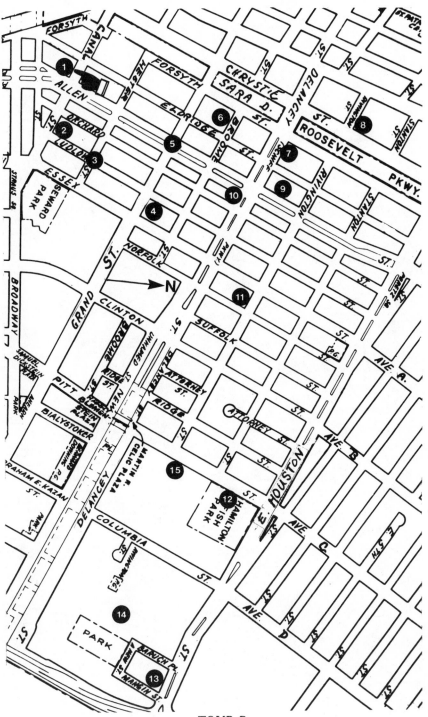

TOUR B

TOUR C

4
The Lower East Side

I can never forget the East Side street where I lived as a boy.

It was a block from the notorious Bowery, a tenement canyon hung with fire-escapes, bed-clothing, and faces.

Always these faces at the tenement windows. The street never failed them. It was an immense excitement. It never slept. It roared like a sea. It exploded like fireworks.

People pushed and wrangled in the street. There were armies of howling pushcart peddlers. Women screamed, dogs barked and copulated. Babies cried....

The Jews had fled from the European pogroms; with prayer, thanksgiving and solemn faith from a new Egypt into a new Promised Land.

They found awaiting them the sweatshops, the bawdy houses and Tammany Hall.

—Michael Gold,
Jews Without Money

The Lower East Side has been the first home for wave after wave of new arrivals. Irish, Italians, Jews, free Blacks, Asians, and Latinos—all hoping to climb America's social and economic ladder. This area, the bottom rung of that ladder, continues to provide volunteers and conscripts for the army of the unskilled.

Physically, the Lower East Side is a mixture of old tenements and high-rise apartment complexes. The projects, which started to go up in the 1930s, are serviceable, though architecturally rather dull.

The traditional flavor of the area is best tasted in the narrow, crowded streets of the old sections. Although the languages have changed several times, the street life has much the same quality it did a century and a half ago. On the faces of the buildings one can see graphic evidence of ethnic change. Synagogues have become churches; Chinese characters half-conceal Roman letters; Spanish covers Yiddish.

Copyright 1974 by Cityarts Workshop Inc., Artistic Director: Tomie Arai

Wall of Respect for Women: This mural was on an outside wall of the Garden Cafeteria and was obliterated in 1983.

TOUR A   *Settlements and Socialism*

Subway information

Start and finish: East Broadway
Station (IND) F train

A1.   **165 East Broadway** *(at Rutgers Street)*
Until last year this was the site of the Garden Cafeteria, a reasonably priced
eating place with a friendly atmosphere. It has recently been taken over by
new owners, who destroyed all traces of its former atmosphere as they
remodeled. In its early days, the Garden Cafeteria was like a European cafe;
politicos and literati would come here to read the newspapers and discuss
the hot issues. Leon Trotsky is said to have been a patron during World
War I, when he was living in exile in New York.

On one of the building's interior walls was a mural, since devastated
by the misguided redecorators, depicting the Artisans' Market of Hester
Park (now called Seward Park). The park is itself just north of here, past
Straus Square. Artisans' markets were a tradition brought from the Old
Country. Carpenters, housepainters, and other craftsmen would gather
every morning at a particular spot. Local people would bargain for their
services and bring the craftsman home with them to do the work when the
price was settled.

A2.   **The Jewish Daily Forward Building** *(175 East Broadway,*
                                                    near Jefferson Street)
The *Forward* was founded in 1897 by Abraham Cahan, who made it one of
the most important Socialist Party newspapers in the United States and the
largest Yiddish-language paper in the world. Cahan was its editor until his
death in 1951. By that time the *Forward* had become thoroughly reformist,
finally acquiring the nickname among the Communists of "the Jewish
Daily Backward." The paper now has its offices uptown.

The building itself was erected in 1911–12. It quickly became a sort of
Jewish socialist community center, housing a Yiddish theater and the
offices of several unions. While it is now a Chinese church, the *Forward*'s
name can be clearly seen on its facade. Of special interest are four bas relief
heads. On the right is Karl Marx and on the left is Friedrich Engels.
(Yiddish is read from right to left.) The center heads are of Ferdinand
Lassalle, founder of the General Association of German Workers, one of
the ancestors of the German Social Democratic Party, and Wilhelm
Liebnicht, who became a leader of that party.

A3.   **Seward Park Library** *(192 East Broadway, near Jefferson Street)*
This branch of the New York Public Library opened in 1910. In its early
days there were often long lines of working people waiting outside its

The Forward Building

Photo by Diane Neumaier

doors. Until recently it had the largest collection of books in Yiddish in the city; this is now housed in the Donnell Branch.

William H. Seward was governor of New York between 1839 and 1842, a senator from 1850 to the beginning of the Civil War, and then Secretary of State in Lincoln's cabinet. He was both an abolitionist and a supporter of the immigrant poor, an unusual combination in·those times.

A4.   The Educational Alliance   *(197 East Broadway,*
near Jefferson Street)

This organization was established in 1889 for the purpose of Americanizing newly arrived East European Jewish immigrants. It was founded by wealthy German Jews whose families had arrived two generations earlier. Their motivation was both self-serving and altruistic. The poor, uneducated East Europeans were something of an embarrassment to the more sophisticated and urbane Germans, and there was always the danger that their "foreign" ways might provoke anti-Semitism. On the other hand, the newcomers were fellow Jews who needed help in adapting to the ways of this strange new country.

The primary emphasis of the Alliance was on uplifting the immigrants via citizenship education and English-language classes. Over the years its social services have increased in response to changing community requirements. The majority of its present clientele are Latino, Asian, and Black, reflecting the population shift in the neighborhood.

Many illustrious speakers have appeared on the stage of the Educational Alliance auditorium. Here Mark Twain met Sholom Aleichem. The former is supposed to have said that he was "happy to meet the Yiddish Mark Twain"; to which the latter is alleged to have replied that he "was glad to make the acquaintance of the English Sholom Aleichem."

A5.   **The Bialystoker Home for the Aged** *(228 and 230 East*
Broadway, near
Clinton Street)

The home consists of two adjacent buildings: a handsome old one (#230) and an ugly, deteriorating new one (#228). The redeeming feature of the latter is the Jewish ethnic mural on its side wall, which is, unfortunately, beginning to deteriorate. It shows the recent history of the Jews, concentrating on union struggles (especially in the garment industry), immigration to the United States, the Holocaust, and the birth of Israel.

In keeping with the *landsmen* tradition (see Lower East Side B2), the home was established by Jewish immigrants from the Polish city of Bialystok. Those worthy citizens also brought us the "bialy," a bread roll something like an onion bagel without the hole.

A6.   **263, 265, 267 Henry Street** *(near Gouverneur Street)*

These are the three original buildings of the Henry Street Settlement, now designated landmark buildings. The settlement was organized in 1893 through the efforts of Lillian Wald, an energetic and devoted nurse and social worker, who enlisted the aid of wealthy Jewish philanthropists, notably Jacob Schiff, in her project. Unlike the Educational Alliance, with its emphasis on uplifting individuals and launching them into the American mainstream, Henry Street was concerned primarily with "the survival and evolution of the individual *and* the survival and evolution of the community and society." The term "settlement" meant that the staff—teachers, nurses, and social workers—settled in the neighborhood and shared in its life. The director and most of the staff still live in the neighborhood. The Henry Street Settlement supports a large number of social services in various locations on the Lower East Side.

In February 1909, responding to a rash of violent acts against Blacks, a group of white and Black liberals and socialists met here and formed the National Negro Committee, out of which grew the National Association for the Advancement of Colored People. The NAACP was the most radical antiracist organization of its time. Its program called for: abolition of all forced segregation; equal educational opportunity; achievement of voting rights; and enforcement of the Fourteenth and Fifteenth Amendments—

the voting rights, due process, and equal protection amendments. The militant tone of the NAACP was established by Dr. W.E.B. Du Bois, editor of its journal, the *Crisis*, in its very first issue:

> Agitation is a necessary evil to tell of the ills of the suffering. Without it many a nation has been lulled to false security and preened itself with virtues it did not possess.
>
> The function of this Association is to tell this nation the crying evil of race prejudice. It is a hard duty but a necessary one—a divine one. It is Pain; Pain is not good but Pain is necessary. Pain does not aggravate disease—Disease causes Pain. Agitation does not mean Aggravation—Aggravation calls for Agitation in order that Remedy be found.

(For more on Dr. Du Bois, see Lower East Side B12.)

Henry Street, as well as Rutgers Street, was named for Henry Rutgers, a pioneer in free public education. The land from which Henry Street was carved was deeded to the city by Rutgers, provided that it build a public school on it before 1811. The school was completed in 1810.

A7.   275 East Broadway *(near Pitt Street)*

This is the site of the now-demolished residence of Meyer London, the first Socialist congressman from the eastern part of the United States. London served from 1915 to 1922, except for the two-year period 1919–20. He had been a labor lawyer who acted on behalf of many of the newly formed unions in the clothing industry. He gave his time and expertise unstintingly, often without pay. When the victorious settlement of the furriers' strike of 1912 was announced, thousands of workers gathered here and compelled him, with their cheers, to address them. When he died in 1926, tens of thousands of mourners followed his coffin from here to the *Forward* building.

Across the street is Samuel Dickstein Plaza. Dickstein was the Tammany hack who was the beneficiary of the bipartisan effort to rid Congress of the baneful influence of Meyer London. The republicrats and demagogues in the state legislature gerrymandered the district in 1922. This deft surgery, the only operation of its kind in the country that year, sliced away a large chunk of London's Socialist support. The major parties then combined forces to back a single candidate: Samuel Dickstein. During the 1930s Dickstein crowned an undistinguished career by godfathering the HUAC (House Committee on Un-American Activities).

In the plaza in front of the Dry Dock Savings Bank is a plaque that quotes one George Jacob Holyoake, a nineteenth-century British reformer, to the effect that society can arrange for "a diffusion of wealth" and yet "touch no man's fortune"—a neat trick. Meyer London's attitude was quite different. In his first speech as a congressman, he said, "I believe in an income tax but I also believe in an inheritance tax that would make it impossible for unfit men by the mere accident of birth to inherit millions of dollars in wealth and power."

A8.   The Henry Street Settlement and Neighborhood Playhouse
(466 Grand Street, at the corner of Pitt Street)

This complex houses many classrooms and three theater spaces. The focus of the playhouse productions is on new plays and readings in Black and Latino theater. On the wall facing Pitt Street is an apparently incomplete mural called *Arise from Oppression* (1972), depicting men and women of all races climbing out of the rubble of broken buildings.

Pitt Street was named for the First Earl of Chatham, William Pitt (see Financial District B5). Americans looked upon him as a friend because of his opposition to British colonial taxation. But a good case can be made that he was merely a wise imperialist who foresaw that if the British pushed too hard, they would lose everything.

A9.   Willett Street

Marinus Willett was a member of the Sons of Liberty prior to the American Revolution. In 1775 he participated in two guerrilla raids, liberating British arms for subsequent use (see Financial District A8).

After the Revolution, Willett was sheriff of New York from 1784 to 1788 and again from 1792 to 1796. Between these two terms he negotiated a treaty with the Creek Indians. Later he turned down a commission as a brigadier-general because it would have meant fighting Indians, something his conscience wouldn't allow. He ended his public career by serving as New York's mayor in 1807.

A10.   Co-op Supermarket *(551 Grand Street, near Jackson Street)*

This store is part of Co-op Village, a complex of housing developments that includes Amalgamated, Hillman, East River, and Seward Park Houses. The Rochdale Pioneers originated the cooperative idea in England in the 1840s. In essence, the principle is to pool financial resources and eliminate profits in order to reduce prices.

In the 1930s the Amalgamated Clothing Workers, under the leader-ship of Sidney Hillman, began an ambitious program of sponsoring cooperative housing in Manhattan. In the 1950s the idea was extended to consumer goods with the establishment of the Co-op Supermarkets. The Twin Pines symbol came to represent low prices and decent quality in both food and housing.

Food co-ops in the city are not confined to the Twin Pines stores. Many smaller ones exist, some of which keep their prices down by asking that members contribute labor as well as money to the enterprise. (see East Village B8.)

A11. **East River Park** *(between Cherry and Jackson Streets)*
If you cross the FDR Drive overpass from Corlears Hook Park, you will come upon a modern-day ruin. This amphitheater was the site of the first Free-Shakespeare-in-the-Park productions, which Joseph Papp began in 1956, initially funded out of his own pocket. Papp was working at the time for CBS and much of his salary was plowed into this project. Two years later, when CBS attempted to fire him because he had invoked the Fifth Amendment before HUAC, he filed a grievance and won. Subsequently he quit CBS to go into the theater business full-time. His venture has expanded into the complex known as the Public Theater (see East Village A5). Free Shakespeare has moved to Central Park, and still flourishes as a summer tradition.

At Corlears Hook on the night of February 25, 1643, 100 Native Americans were attacked and massacred, on order of the Dutch governor, for having the temerity to resist taxation.

A12. **Su Casa Drug Rehabilitation Center** *(9 Gouverneur Slip East, near Water Street)*
Inside the building is a circular stairway, the entire length of which has a painted mural entitled *The Transition*. It illustrates the development of self-awareness and self-respect through mutual support and encouragement. Please ask for permission before viewing the mural.

Gouverneur Slip is named for Abraham Gouverneur, who was a political ally of Jacob Leisler (see Civic Center/Lower West Side A4). When Leisler was arrested and charged with treason, Gouverneur fled to Boston. His flight saved his life, for both of them were sentenced to death. Leisler was executed in 1691, and Gouverneur devoted the next decade to clearing their names.

A13. **P.S. 137** *(Cherry Street, between Montgomery and Clinton Streets)*
On the side wall of this school near Clinton Street is an unusual mural. While most of the Lower East Side murals convey an optimistic revolutionary message, this one is a violently nihilistic representation of doomsday. And unlike the others, this one has unleashed a graffitic dialogue about the mural itself rather than the more typical scrawled names and initials.

A14. **La Guardia Houses** *(Madison Street at Jefferson Street)*
This project is named for New York's progressive mayor, Fiorello La Guardia, who served from 1934 to 1945. The "Little Flower," who defeated Tammany and gave New York its best administration in a century, was well loved by its citizens. While a congressman, he was coauthor of the Norris-La Guardia Act (1932), which helped fledgling unions to organize.

In the park of the housing development is a mural entitled *Puerto Rico, Isla de Encanto*. It is a bright, colorful depiction of life in Puerto Rico, contrasting bitterly with the very building on which it appears. To the uninitiated, this mural may appear to be mere decoration. But, in fact, it features the first flag of Puerto Rican independence from Spain and the visage of Pedro Alizu Campos, a leader of the Puerto Rican independence movement in the 1920s.

Madison Street, named for our fourth president and one of the principal authors of the Constitution, had until 1826 been called Bancker Street, after a socially prominent eighteenth-century family. When the Banckers decided that the neighborhood was going to the dogs, the family had the name changed.

In 1806, a year before the first public school was established (see Lower East Side C9), the Free School Society founded a nonreligious school for the children of the poor. It met in an apartment on this street and in its first year served some 40 students.

A15.   Rutgers Community Center   *(200 Madison Street, off Rutgers Street)*

Inside this building, in the gym to the right, is a striking mural showing the Indian/Spanish culture and the African culture meeting in the person of a triumphant boxer. The Cityarts catalog says: "It depicts the culture and the history of the teenagers who designed and painted it." (For more on Cityarts see East Village A3.)

The center is open from 8 A.M. to 5 P.M. during the summer (when school is out) and from 2 P.M. to 10 P.M. during the rest of the year.

A16.   191 Madison Street *(between Rutgers and Pike Streets)*

On the Pike Street side of this building is a mural entitled *Chi Lai/Arriba/ Rise Up!* (1974). It is a powerful depiction of U.S. imperialism's imprisonment of Asians, Latinos, and Blacks as they struggle to break out of their confinement.

TOUR B   *A Century of Tenement Life*

Subway information

Start and finish: Delancey Street
Station (IND) F train

B1.   54–58 Canal Street *(near Allen Street)*

Here stands the Jarmulovsky's Bank building. Its clientele was drawn mostly from the neighborhood: poor immigrants who saved pennies in the hopes of bringing their families from the old country. As World War I approached, there was a great rush to help relatives escape from Europe. This rush became a panic when rumors of the bank's insolvency began to circulate. Street riots erupted as desperate people tried to force their way into the building. On "Black Tuesday," August 4, 1914, the bank closed and

Chi Lai/Arriba/Rise Up

thousands lost their life's savings. The bank's owners were brought to trial. The punishment: suspended sentences.

The shell of the bank still stands intact, with its name and the date of its founding (1873) carved on the corner doorway.

B2.   5 **Ludlow Street** *(near Canal Street)*
This building was erected in 1892 by the Independent Kletzker Brotherly Aid Society. Immigrant groups often banded together by nationality, forming mutual aid societies from which members could draw both financial and social benefits. They were organized on the basis of Old World ties and often bore the names of their villages of origin or perhaps of the patron saint of a village. Thus, the Kletzker Society was made up of Jewish *landsmen* from the Polish village of Kletzk. You can see the name of the society near the top of the facade. (Around the corner, at 41 Canal Street, is a building very similar in architectural style, with its facade removed. Very probably this was another such society.)

Across the street from this handsome old building is an undistinguished and paternalistic mural put up by the 7th Police Precinct Youth Council. Form and content are consistent: the colors are dull and the figures crudely drawn.

Ludlow Street was formerly the site of a debtors' prison, whose most famous—and infamous—inmate was Boss Tweed, who died there on April 12, 1878 (see Civic Center/Lower West Side A10).

B3. **Ludlow and Hester Streets**
Around the turn of the century, before unions developed, there was a daily shapeup here. Hiring agents arrived early in the morning to pick work crews for the day. The commotion caused by the yelling and jostling of hundreds of people pressing into this narrow intersection accounts for its being called *chazer* market. (The *ch* in *chazer* is pronounced as in the German *ach*; it means "pig.")

During the days of the *chazer* market, this was the center of the garment district. While most of the garment business has since moved uptown, there are still tiny factories operating very near here, in Chinatown, where people work under conditions resembling those of a century ago (see Lower East Side C1).

B4. **Seward Park High School** *(Ludlow Street between Grand and Broome Streets)*
Inside the auditorium of the school may be seen paintings in the style typical of public art projects produced by the WPA in the 1930s. These

noble, inspirational figures, now covered with decades of grime, are symbols of an educational philosophy that was built on the veneration of inherited truth.

During the turbulent 1960s, when students were rebelling, the authorities at Seward Park High School took measures. A law-enforcement brigade stood guard in the halls to prevent students from cutting classes and raided the bathrooms to flush out smokers. They were complemented by narcotics agents disguised as janitors. In November 1968, during a citywide student strike, some 30 tactical police slept inside the building. The public address system spoke in code: "Immediate meeting of the standing committee" meant that students were to be kept where they were until further notice. They received an education, but it wasn't in reading, writing, or 'rithmetic.

B5.   Grand and Allen Streets
In December 1907, with 125,000 unemployed in New York City, a mass meeting was held here to inaugurate a rent strike. Although a month later the strike had succeeded in achieving rent reductions for 2,000 families, many were still being dispossessed. The city hired a squad of unemployed men to remove these tenants' belongings from the buildings. But what did those ungrateful irregulars do? They refused to work without an increase in wages and announced that they had formed a "Furniture Snatchers' Organization" to press their demands!

B6.   Broome and Forsyth Streets
In 1872 a building at this location housed the headquarters of the International Workingmen's Association—the First International. It had been founded in September 1864 in London and was led by Marx and Engels. Its purpose was to provide the organizational structure for implementing international solidarity among workers. We haven't been able to pinpoint the building, but we would like to think it is the one on the south side of the street that has a new coat of red paint on its windows.

Some fifty years earlier, in 1829, Broome Street was the home of the Hall of Science, sponsored by the followers of Robert Owen, a utopian socialist. The Owenites bought an old church and remodeled it for use as a school and lecture hall. They also put out their journal the *Free Enquirer* from here.

The park that extends from Houston to Canal Streets between Chrystie and Forsyth Streets is named for Sara Delano Roosevelt, the mother of FDR. Undoubtedly that patrician lady would be scandalized at the association of her name with this devastated piece of real estate. However, despite its dirt and dereliction, it is well-used by the children of the neighborhood.

Seeds for Progressive Change

Copyright 1975 by Cityarts Workshop, Inc., Artistic Director: Alfredo Hernandez
This photograph was taken before the mural was defaced.

In the park at Broome Street is a 1982 mural by Jimmy P., Ralph H., Milton O., Vinny N., and Pablo D., saying

Our Father
Forgive those who can't respect this park. . . . ., it is gone,
Forgive those who sleep on this floor. . . . ., until dawn,
Forgive those who play on the sand. . . . . all full of glass,
Forgive those who bring the ladies of the night. . . . . . ., no . . . no-touch-
of-class

This is put in the mouth of a youth near a sign saying "Keep this park clean!" Between the building and Forsyth Street is a small, well-tended garden, whose flowers are there for all to see, since people have honored the sign saying not to pick them.

B7.   Delancey and Forsyth Streets
Delancey Street is named for Étienne De Lancey, one of the wealthy Tories who owned vast tracts of land in the city. His holdings stretched from the Bowery to the East River and from Stanton Street south to Division Street. After the Revolution he lost his land and fled the country. Although nearly all the Royalist names in the city were replaced, De Lancey's remained.

At Forsyth Street may be found the mural *Seeds for a Progressive Change*, another Cityarts project. This one was painted in 1975 and depicts Puerto Rican life: education, work, and cooperation. Prominently featured is a large banner issuing from the sewing machine of a working woman, bearing the legend "Viva Puerto Rico Libre." The Cityarts catalog informs us that:

> Portraits of Ho Chi Minh, Malcolm X, and Lolita Lebron were
> included. . . . Soon after its completion, the mural was defaced and the
> portraits were covered with white paint. The mural members decided to
> leave the defacement as is, thereby making a statement to the community
> who would be viewing it daily.

B8.   Rivington and Chrystie Streets
A mural here, *New Birth* (1974), portrays the Native American and the wilderness on one side and the "dragon" of technology on the other. In the middle is a synthesis of the two—a new birth.

New Birth was the first Cityarts mural to include local community involvement. "Prior to painting," says the Cityarts catalog, "the mock-up was circulated throughout the neighborhood and approved and added to by the local residents."

*B9.   133 **Allen Street** (off Delancey Street)*
This Municipal Bath House was built in 1905. The first of these free public facilities, sponsored by the New York Association for Improving the Condition of the Poor, opened in 1852. In its first year of operation nearly 100,000 people who lived in cold-water flats made use of its services. The bath house here, one of the last remaining, is open every day except Mondays and holidays for the use of those who are still without hot water. As recently as 1970, more than 44,000 apartments in Manhattan did not have full plumbing facilities.

*B10.   **Allen and Delancey Streets** (southeast corner)*
This imposing edifice was at one time occupied by the Bank of the United States, a rather grandiose title considering its fate. The bank was largely Jewish-owned, and when it failed in 1932 it was rumored that several large banks had conspired to deny it short-term credit, contrary to common practice. If you look hard you can make out its name on the Delancey Street facade.

On the Allen Street side of the building, at eye-level, is the mural *Art as an Alternative to Violence*. Painted in 1974 by a team from the neighborhood Youth Corps, it was designed by a single artist under the auspices of Cityarts, and bears the legend: "It is the job of the enlightened to rebuild with the tools of creativity, what the hateful, with their weapons of oppression, have destroyed."

*B11.   127 **Rivington Street** (at Norfolk Street)*
In the late nineteenth century this was the site of Eisl's Golden Rule Hall. On July 7, 1882, during a longshoremen's strike, a meeting was held here, sponsored by the Propaganda Association for the Dissemination of Socialist Ideas Among Immigrant Jews to persuade the newcomers not to scab on their fellow workers, most of whom were Irish and German.

Newly arrived greenhorns of all nationalities needed above all a job, a place to sleep, and something to eat. Many had little experience as workers and no idea of the dynamics of labor-management relations. Needless to say, they had no conception of what scabbing was, and were often recruited as strikebreakers right off the boat. The newly developing labor movement and its Socialist allies took great pains to educate them—and they learned quickly. On July 14, for instance, a shipload of 500 Jews was persuaded to march straight from the Battery to union headquarters. The very next day, 250 Italian immigrants left off scabbing at the New York Central Railroad Yard and joined up.

This strike marked the beginnings of socialist influence in New York City trade unionism, which led to the Eight-Hour Day movement, the annual Labor Day celebration, and the emergence of the needle trades unions.

(The next four entries are somewhat out of the way, but we believe they are worth the extra walk.)

B12.   Hamilton Fish Play Center *(Pitt Street off Stanton Street)*
During the summer this park features an outdoor swimming pool. At some hours kids can swim for free; the rest of the time it costs a mere dime. Look inside the building to see the line that the kids have to be taller than in order to be able to get in alone.

Mobilization for Youth, which did good work in community organization in the 1960s, had its headquarters across the street. Up the block is a branch of the Boys' Club. Richard Nixon, during one of his more bizarre excursions into paranoia, accused the Du Bois Clubs (a Communist youth organization pronounced "D Boys") of choosing its name to ensnare the beardless members of the Silent Majority.

Since Du Bois campaigned for peace, he was one of those "Soviet agents" upon whom Nixon was anxious to tread on his way to the U.S. throne. But when Du Bois was tried in 1951 for "failure to register as a foreign agent," he was acquitted. Du Bois spent his long life fighting for Negro rights and African unity. He joined the Communist Party in 1961 at the age of 93.

B13.   P.S. 97 *(Houston Street and Mangin Street)*
On the school's side wall is a mural entitled *Por Los Niños*, painted in 1976 by students in response to cutbacks in educational programs. It shows at the bottom a form of hell: the degradation of children through drugs and prostitution. Above this rises a pyramid of books: art, music, history, science, English, math. At the top, a "magic lamp" produces artists, professionals, and workers. The message is both moving and sad, for the schools continue to deteriorate, and the "magic lamp" has failed to provide an escape from the ghetto.

B14.   Baruch Houses *(Houston Street to Delancey Street, Columbia Street to FDR Drive)*
Baruch Houses is named for Dr. Simon Baruch (the father of Bernard, pal of presidents). His concern for the health of the poor led Baruch to campaign for public bath houses; one such bath house was built here while this was still a tenement neighborhood.

In the middle of the project, south of the playground, is the Dr. Simon Baruch Recreation Center. The building is totally derelict. When we came through the area with our notebooks and pencils, some kids who were playing nearby—mistaking us, no doubt, for minor bureaucrats—ran up and asked hopefully whether we were "going to fix the building."

B15.   **Grand Street Settlement** *(80 Pitt Street, between Stanton and Rivington Streets)*

The Grand Street Settlement was founded in 1916. (For more on settlement houses, see Lower East Side A6.) Today it offers a full program of day-care, Headstart, art classes, English-language classes, and special activities for old people. It is a busy, well-kept building. Take a look at the mural on the landing between the first and second floors, entitled *The World of Africa*. It was created by children in a woodworking class.

The settlement is on the grounds of the Samuel Gompers Houses, named after the first president of the American Federation of Labor, an advocate of the conservative, craft union approach to organization. His antisocialist orientation still dominates U.S. trade unionism.

TOUR C   *Chinatown/Little Italy*

Subway information

Start and finish: Canal Street
Station (IRT) #4, #5, or #6 train

C1.   **5th Precinct Police Station** *(19–21 Elizabeth Street, between Bayard and Canal Streets)*

On June 30, 1975, there was a demonstration here by Chinese residents protesting police brutality and harassment. The police response was to club a dozen protestors to the ground. This demonstration, part of a campaign led by Asian Americans for Equal Employment, grew out of an incident in late April when a 27-year-old architectural engineer was stripped and beaten inside the station house. As a result of the protests, the commanding officer of the 5th Precinct was transferred.

On October 19, 1979, the *New York Times* published a list of almost 90 sweatshops operating in Chinatown, including two that flanked this very station house: Cheung Lee Sportswear at #15 and Modern Modes at #25. These factories employed Chinese laborers at wages far below legal minimum. The Labor Department found it almost impossible to obtain evidence. As is the case with most undocumented labor, the bosses keep quiet to maximize profits and the workers keep quiet out of fear of deportation.

C2.   **Transfiguration Catholic Church**   *(29 Mott Street, near Pell Street)*

During the 1930s this church was the scene of an important development in the Chinese resistance to racism. For decades, Chinese had been frozen out of the mainstream of the U.S. economy, being confined to the restaurant and hand-laundry businesses.

When fierce competition developed between the hand laundries and the mechanized chain laundries, the response of the Chinese was to add services, such as free mending. The chains' strategy was to destroy the hand laundries by taking away their customers. They displayed placards showing buck-toothed, pigtailed "Chinamen" dampening shirts by spitting on them.

After the placards were removed, thanks to the intervention of the Chinese consul-general, the chains lobbied to have the city council pass a law mandating a $1,000 bond from owners of laundries, knowing that most hand-laundry owners could not begin to raise such a sum. Finally, in April 1933, the small shopowners held a meeting in the basement of this church that led to a successful campaign to prevent passage of the bill. Out of this triumph was born the Chinese Hand-Laundry Alliance.

The alliance was concerned with the world situation as well as local affairs. Its official representative was elected to the executive committee of the U.S. National Democratic and Peace Congress, a progressive antifascist organization that supported the Republicans during the Spanish Civil War. After World War II, the alliance sent a message to President Truman opposing U.S. intervention in the Chinese Civil War, thus supporting the communists.*

It is impossible to write about Chinatown without noting that it has what must be the highest density of restaurants in the world. Most of them offer good food at moderate prices.

C3.   **Baxter, Worth, and Park Streets**

In the nineteenth century the irregular intersection formed by these streets was called Five Points. It was one of the most poverty-stricken and demoralized parts of the city. The center of the neighborhood was the Old

---

*Before this area became known as Chinatown, it was the center of Little Africa. Chinese immigrants began settling here in the 1850s, but it wasn't until the 1880s that large numbers began to arrive, fleeing the violent racism of the West, where the states were attempting to engineer the removal of the Chinese after their usefulness on railroad construction crews had ended. In 1890 the Chinese population in New York was 2,500; by 1920 it had doubled. Another large increase in immigration began in 1965, when the United States lifted its "national origins" quota. Within five years the Chinese population had increased to 69,000.

Brewery, where prostitutes and thugs hung out. Charles Dickens, who visited here in 1842, wrote, "Women and men slink off to sleep, forcing the dislodged rats to move away." At least 10,000 homeless children squatted here, some making pennies as newsboys or bootblacks, most living by their wits—begging or indulging in petty thievery. Street gangs flourished, with picturesque names and political connections.

Around Five Points lived the white poor, joined in the 1820s by increasing numbers of freed slaves. In the 1830s it was the scene of the first major outbreak of that chronic U.S. disease, racism. Perceiving Blacks as competitors in the job market, whites precipitated a series of race riots, one of which was the Chatham Street riot. Identifying the wealthy abolitionists with their oppressors, they became increasingly attracted by the siren song of Tammany Hall, the "friend of the poor" and dispenser of petty patronage and political muscle.

By the end of the century, Tammany was in decline, the street gangs had been destroyed, and the infamous brewery had been demolished. Now, Five Points is just another intersection with only a parking lot to mark the spot.

To the north is Columbus Park, the site of the notorious Mulberry Bend tenements. Jacob Riis, that compassionate chronicler of the poor, noted in 1882 that while the city's death rate was 46.2 per thousand, this block had a death rate of 68.3. Such blocks were referred to as "lung blocks." Tuberculosis was rampant here, aggravated by lack of sunlight and poor air circulation, attacking bodies already weakened from laboring long hours in airless lofts. Middle-class support for tearing down the slums was not entirely selfless; it feared the spread of tuberculosis to its own neighborhoods. Mulberry Bend was torn down in 1895 and the park constructed on the site.

In the 1880s Mulberry Street, between Bayard and Park Streets, was the center of Little Italy. It is now part of Chinatown, but one or two Italian names may still be seen on its store fronts.

C4.   Park Row *(between Pearl and Worth Streets)*

In the eighteenth century there existed a well here, known as the Tea-water Pump. It was the only well in Manhattan that produced good water; all the others contained water that even horses refused to drink. The trucks that stopped here to fill their casks caused mile-long traffic jams (a foretaste of the future). It was this water shortage that led Aaron Burr to dream up his clever bank scheme. (See Financial District B8.)

Park Row was formerly called Chatham Street, for William Pitt, Earl of Chatham (see Lower East Side A8). (The nearby square is still known as Chatham Square.) At one time there was a Chatham Street Chapel on this block. On October 2, 1833, a tiny band of abolitionists met there to form an

Cartoon by Art Young

antislavery society. Outside, a raging mob, having learned of their intentions, attempted to break into the chapel. The abolitionists escaped by a back door and the mob vented its rage by destroying the furniture. A Black man, whom they attempted to intimidate, delivered a diatribe against slavery, quoting the Bible and the Declaration of Independence.

C5.   New York Telephone Company Building *(Pearl Street and St. James Place)*

The sleek anonymity of this edifice gives no hint of its origins. In 1970 the site was home to more than two dozen Chinese families. In order to expedite corporate "progress," the families were evicted and the houses marked for demolition. Soon afterward nearly all the families moved back in illegally, attempting to prevent the destruction of their homes. They were led by the We Won't Move Out But We Will Move In Committee. But in the end their courage and resolve were no match for the power of New York Tel.

C6.   Alfred E. Smith Houses *(Catherine Street, near Cherry Street)*

In a small park off Catherine Street is a statue of Al Smith, governor of New York from 1919 to 1928. At one time there was a New York City employment office here. During the summer of 1953, 7,500 people responded to a notice of city job vacancies. Some were so desperate that they camped out in the park for almost a week. Luckily for them it was summertime. Unluckily for 97 percent of them, there were only 180 openings.

C7.   New York Post Building *(Water Street, between Catherine Slip and Market Slip)*

On the back of the building is *The Italian Mural* (1974). It is the result of the combined effort of Cityarts and the community of Little Italy. The Cityarts brochure says: "The mural is a series of 6 panels depicting the problems facing the people in the neighborhood, and their aspiration for a more united community."

C8.   Knickerbocker Village *(Monroe, Market, Cherry, and Catherine Streets)*

This project was built in 1934 by the Metropolitan Life Insurance Company, replacing a cluster of squalid tenements. While it was a good idea to take down the slums, this urban renewal was in reality urban removal. With rents in the new project more than double those of the surrounding neighborhood, most who had lived here were compelled to move away. On top of this, Metropolitan Life instituted a Whites-Only

Ollie Harrington, *The Daily World.* Reprinted by permission.

policy. As late as 1953 it succeeded in evicting the sole Black family that had slipped through its nets. This policy is now illegal.

On the top floor of 10 Monroe Street there lived in 1950 a young family—mother, father, and two boys. In the summer of that year both parents were arrested. The consequences of those arrests shattered the family and left their mark on the whole world. The names of the arrested were Julius and Ethel Rosenberg.

C9.   P.S. 1 *(Henry Street between Catherine and Oliver Streets)*
This building is a typical example of turn-of-the-century school design. Notice, for instance, the separate girls' and boys' entrances and the street signs carved on the building's corners. Inside the main entrance is a plaque describing the erection of the school in 1897–98.

This is the "new" P.S. 1. The original, situated nearby on Park Row, was the first public school in the city, opening its doors on April 28, 1807.

C10.   Books New China *(53 East Broadway, near Market Street)*
While most of the books here are in Chinese, there are some in English, notably revolutionary novels and Marxist classics. The store also carries records, games, toys, crafts, and inexpensive art works.

C11.   19 Eldridge Street *(off Canal Street)*
This triple building was put up in 1879, the year of the city's first Tenement Law. In what was for that era a significant advance, the city required that every habitable room in all new tenements provide access to fresh air. The "dumbbell" was the design model developed to create airshafts for interior rooms.

The building code was updated in 1901 and these houses came to be called "Old Law Tenements." Note the carved heads and other decorative details that distinguish this building from its neighbors.

C12.   Hester, Forsyth, Chrystie, and Canal Streets
In this block stood the Libby Hotel, linked with the immortal Judge Joseph Crater, America's most famous missing person. On August 6, 1930, he vanished in the midst of a grand jury investigation into his shady real estate dealings. In the pocket of one of his suits, investigators found a handwritten memo saying, "Libby Hotel—there will be a very large sum due me for services when the city pays the two and three quarter million dollars in condemnation." The hotel was condemned and disappeared; Judge Crater disappeared and was condemned.

C13. **Hester Street and Bowery**

The mural here is entitled *Wall of Respect for the Working People of Chinatown* (1977). It incorporates the likenesses of parents of many of the young people who painted it. The mural portrays early immigrants, trans-continental railway workers, cooks, waiters, and dressmakers—all enfolded in the curves of the Chinese dragon. It is an expressive and engaging work of art, and although it reaches right to sidewalk level, is unmarred by graffiti.

C14. **137 Mulberry Street** *(near Hester Street)*

In May 1820 the Second African Free School for Boys opened at this address. It was funded by Black and white abolitionists. This area, once part of Little Africa, is now in the heart of Little Italy.

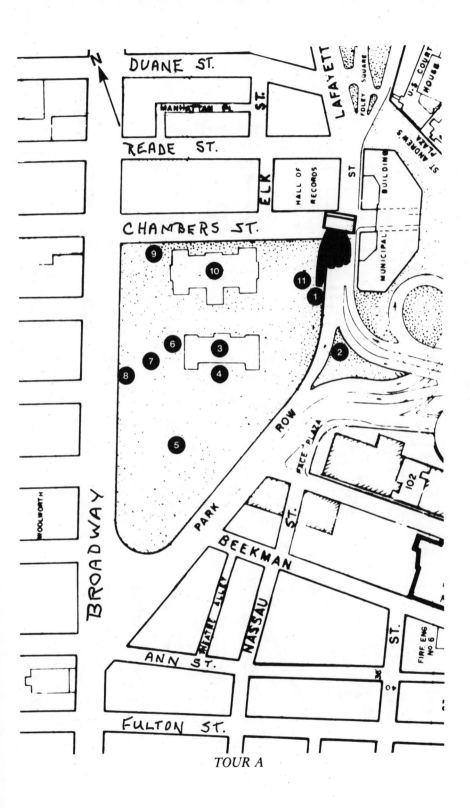

TOUR A

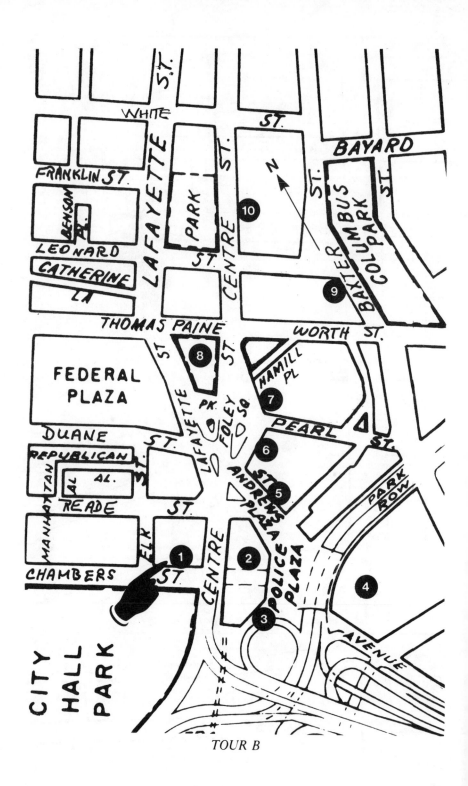

TOUR B

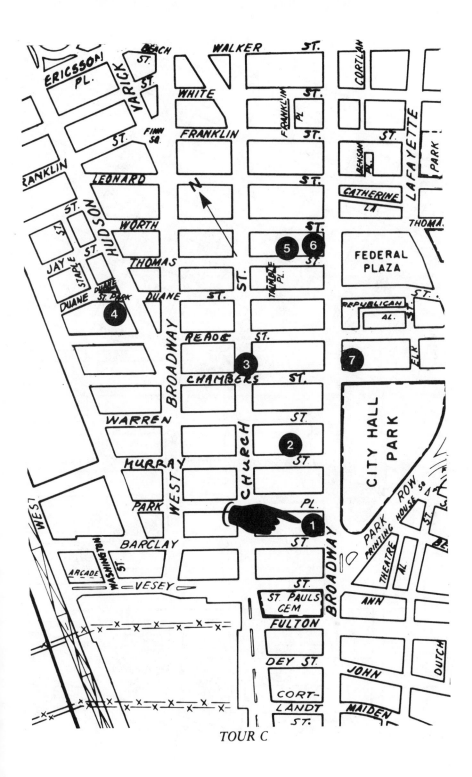

TOUR C

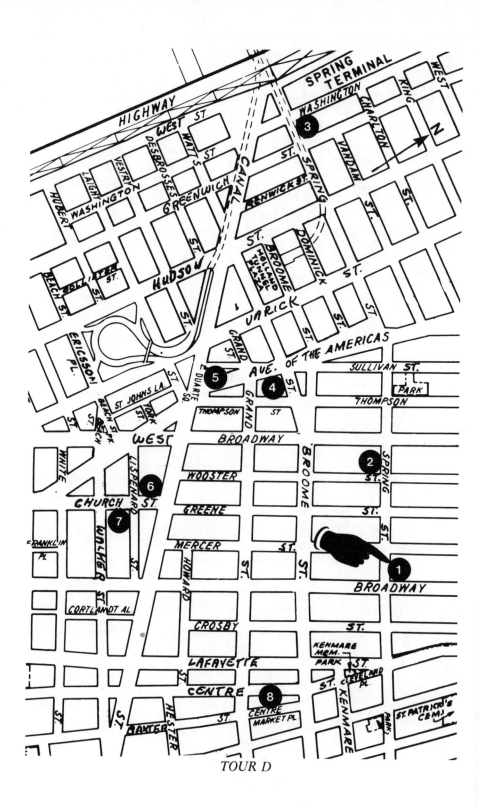

TOUR D

5
Civic Center/
Lower West Side

Go fight City Hall!
—*Unanimous*

This is an area of abrupt contrasts. The Civic Center, to the north of
City Hall, is filled with monumental governmental architecture. Broadway,
immediately to its west, is a commercial street. Still farther west is an area of
warehouses, now in the process of becoming a new artists' quarter: TriBeCa
(the *Tri*angle *Be*low *Ca*nal Street). Canal Street itself is one long flea market;
with lots of patience and some loose change, you can spend hours
inspecting and selecting from its boxes, barrels, and bins.

To the north of Canal Street is SoHo (the area *So*uth of *Ho*uston
Street). The palatial cast-iron factories here were the sweatshops of the late
nineteenth century; the area was a small-industry backwater until it was
discovered by the art community in the 1960s. Unfortunately, struggling
artists are not necessarily political; visitors who seek social commentary in
the lofts and studios of SoHo will be largely disappointed. Nevertheless,
SoHo's craft, clothing, and food shops are a delight to the senses, and its
galleries and performing spaces present a kaleidoscope of avant-garde
art. Since events here are always changing, we suggest you scan the listings
in the *Village Voice* and make up your own route.

TOUR A   Around City Hall

Subway information

Start and finish: Brooklyn Bridge
Station (IRT) #4, #5, or #6 train

A1.   **Brooklyn Bridge Subway Station** *(Lexington Ave./IRT Line)*
This station was the first stop of the first subway line constructed in New
York City, which opened in 1904. (The initial excavation site is marked by a
plaque in front of City Hall.) In 1892, even before ground was broken, a
dispute raged over public versus private ownership of the subways. The
settlement of this controversy is an object lesson in how the government
serves the ruling class. After the city paid for construction, it leased the
completed subway to a private concern, headed by August Belmont. For its
first 35 years the New York subway system was operated by private
entrepreneurs.

Within six months of its opening, the IRT was struck. Workers wanted
a nine-hour day, a limitation of 100 miles per run, and a ten percent wage
increase. Belmont imported a thousand scabs and broke both the strike and
the union. It was three decades before IRT workers organized successfully
(see Financial District C10).

At the foot of the stairs leading out of the station are three large
plaques from the original station. While these honor mayors, engineers,
and, of course, Belmont, not a word is mentioned of the thousands of
workers whose labor built the system, or of the more than a hundred who
died constructing the first 13 miles of tunnel and track.

A2.   **Brooklyn Bridge Approach**
This bridge was the first solid link between New York and Brooklyn, which
was until 1898 an independent city, the third largest in the United States.
John Roebling conceived of the bridge, and his son Washington oversaw its
construction. Much has been made of Roebling Sr.'s tragic death in 1869
while working on the bridge's caissons, and of the crippling injury to his
son three years later. Without belittling their dedication or accomplishment, we feel that a word should be said for the 20 workers who died on
the job. The completion of the Brooklyn Bridge in 1883 furthered the move
toward the incorporation of Greater New York, which was accomplished in
1898.

Once upon a time there was a fable called the Hick who Tried to Buy
the Brooklyn Bridge. Everybody laughed because they knew the bridge
belonged to We, the People. At least it did until 1975, when the fiscal crisis
sent the city up the creek. At which point it sold the bridge, along with the
rest of the city, down the river to the bankers' trust.

Courtesy of Tom Jones/New York Marxist School

A3.   City Hall

The city government moved here from its old home in Lower Manhattan when the building was completed in 1811. It is surprisingly small and in the style of a French chateau, with a domed central hall, symmetrical curved staircases, and crystal chandeliers—an elegant setting for the mayor's office, the Board of Estimate, and the city council.

In 1857 the city's business was disrupted briefly, but spectacularly. The state legislature had abolished the old, corrupt Municipal Police and created a new Metropolitan Police force. When the mayor, Fernando Wood, refused to disband the municipals, the metropolitans were sent to arrest him. This led to a battle royal inside City Hall. Finally, the National

Guard arrived and imposed an uneasy peace while the issue went to court. Mayor Wood lost and the city had a new police force.

Between 1936 and 1947, when the proportional representation system was in effect, minority party candidates were able to be elected to the city council. Two Communists, Peter Cacchione of Brooklyn and Benjamin Davis of Harlem, as well as several members of the left-wing American Labor Party, were influential in the work of the city council. Ultimately, the Democrats, using red-baiting tactics, killed proportional representation and grabbed almost all the seats for themselves. This tyranny of the majority is still operating.

Recently the city council has been agonizing over a reapportionment plan that would broaden minority representation. Several plans have been vetoed by the courts. Nobody has suggested proportional representation. Perhaps they fear a resurgence of the Left?

A4.   **In Front of City Hall**

Even before City Hall was built, this Common figured significantly in the city's history. In 1691 it was the scene of New York's most hideous execution. Jacob Leisler was a captain of the militia and a popular hero. In 1689, when the previous governor was forced to resign, Leisler was persuaded to become interim governor until the arrival of the Crown's new appointee. When a British officer appeared and demanded that Leisler turn over authority to him, Leisler refused, preferring to relinquish this authority to the new governor alone. British troops thereupon besieged the rebel and his supporters and, after two months, forced their surrender.

When the Crown's appointee finally showed up, he had Leisler tried for treason on the grounds that he had fired upon British troops. According to Samuel Eliot Morrison (in the *Oxford History of the American People*), Leisler and his son-in-law "were hanged by the neck, their bodies cut down while still alive, their bowels ripped out and burned before their faces, their heads cut off, and their bodies quartered." Many of his devoted followers labored for years to clear his name, and in 1702 he was finally exonerated (see Lower East Side A12). For generations people identified their political views as Leislerian or anti-Leislerian.

The account of the Leisler affair on the Heritage Trail Marker in front of City Hall does little to elucidate this episode in our history. In fact, by maintaining that there was "grumbling among the populace" over "his heavy-handed rule," it does a disservice to this unsung people's hero and martyr.

In 1735 an Alms House was erected on the Common and in 1775 Bridewell Prison was added. Debtors often languished there for many months because they were unable to repay small sums. One accomplishment of the New York Working Men's Party a half-century later

was the elimination of debt as a crime. Bridewell had the usual comple-
ment of whipping post, stocks, and pillory. The gallows was reserved for
those convicted of capital crimes. These were but three: murder, treason,
and stealing from church.

William Mooney, who founded Tammany Hall in 1789, was a
superintendent of the Alms House. His salary was $1,000 per year plus
$500 for family expenses. When asked how he came to run up bills of more
than $5,000 for "extras," he explained that it was mostly "for trifles for Mrs.
Mooney." Nearly a century later, Boss Tweed elevated the art of creative
appropriation to new and breathtaking heights (see Civic Center/Lower
West Side A10).

A5.   City Hall Park

In 1872 there was a three-month general strike to achieve the eight-hour
day. At a rally here on May 27, Alexander Troup of the National
Typographical Union said:

> We have determined to make eight hours a legal day's work from one end
> of Manhattan to the other. . . . Capitalists say they don't place much
> dependence on the eight-hour system; that they work twelve hours
> themselves. What of it? If they want to work twelve hours, let them. We
> want to work eight hours.*

Two weeks later the strike was won and the eight-hour day achieved.
But it was a short-lived victory. A financial panic the next year caused
massive unemployment and threw the workers' movement into disarray—
and the eight-hour day was lost.

In February 1936, during the Great Depression, a march of the
unemployed ended with a rally here. The city fathers had refused them a
permit, but they marched anyway and some were arrested. One of those
arrested was a freshman congressman who had just addressed the rally:
Vito Marcantonio, then a Republican, later a leader of the American Labor
Party. The cops were embarrassed to discover an employed congressman
among the unemployed malcontents. They tried to get rid of him but he
refused to leave, demanding, "let my comrades go, too." After several hours
of jousting he won and all were freed.

On May 20, 1970, employers and labor bureaucrats joined forces to
manufacture a huge pro-Vietnam War demonstration. The bosses gave the
workers paid time off, on condition that they attend the demonstration.
To guarantee attendance, their labor lieutenants provided roll-call sheets.

---

*M.R. Werner, *It Happened in New York* (New York: Coward, McCann, 1957).

The next day, 40,000 workers and students replied. In a hastily organized demonstration, they assembled at City Hall to protest the escalation of the war and the killings at Jackson State College and Kent State University.

At the southern tip of the park is a fountain, built after a massive post office was demolished in 1938. In April 1918 the post office was the scene of the trial of the editorial board of the *Masses*, a revolutionary literary and arts magazine that was at the center of left-wing cultural life before World War I. As a result of opposition to the war, its entire editorial board was accused of "conspiring to promote insubordination and mutiny in the military and naval forces of the United States and to obstruct the recruitment and enlistment to the injury of the service."

On the first day of the trial, a brass band, which happened to be stationed near a liberty bond booth just under the post office windows, began to play "The Star-Spangled Banner." One of the defendants leaped to his feet. The judge could not ignore this patriotic display and rose also, followed by the entire courtroom. After this gymnastic routine had repeated itself four times, the exasperated judge finally called a halt. Many believed the defendants had planned the charade in advance, when in fact it was an inspired improvisation. The trial ended with a hung jury, as did the retrial, leaving the defendants free to resume publication.

A6.   Isaac Barré Memorial Plaque
Barré was a British politician who opposed taxation of the colonies, and whose term "sons of liberty" was adopted by the militants of the Revolutionary period. These Sons of Liberty took the lead in demonstrating against British colonial policies in the decade leading to the Revolution. In response to the passage of the Stamp Act in 1765, for instance, they raised a gibbet in this Common and hanged the British governor in effigy. They formed a torchlight procession to Battery Park and thence to the governor's house, where they seized his carriage, tore down the wooden fence surrounding Bowling Green, and set fire to the whole lot.

A7.   Liberty Pole
In March 1766 the Stamp Act was repealed, and on the first anniversary of its repeal, a "liberty pole" was raised on the Common. It was made of white pine, the tree reserved by the Crown for ships of the British Navy. Its erection so inflamed the British that they hacked it down immediately. Another was put up the next day, which was also chopped down. On the following day, 3,000 people held a protest meeting in the Common and defiantly set up a third pole. Again the British destroyed it. Perhaps foreseeing the annihilation of the white pine supply, the British left a

fourth liberty pole standing. When they finally toppled it on January 17, 1770, the action precipitated the Battle of Golden Hill (see Financial District D7). The flagpole on the Green, west of City Hall, commemorates the liberty poles—symbols of American defiance of British colonial rule.

On July 9, 1776, with George Washington in attendance, the citizens of New York assembled on this Common to hear for the first time the words of that brilliant anti-imperialist call to resistance, the Declaration of Independence.

> We hold these truths to be self-evident, that all men are created equal, that they are endowed by their Creator with certain unalienable Rights, that among these are Life, Liberty and the pursuit of Happiness; That to secure these rights, Governments are instituted among Men, deriving their just powers from the consent of the governed; That whenever any Form of Government becomes destructive of these ends, it is the Right of the People to alter or abolish it, and to institute new Government. ... That these United Colonies are, and of Right ought to be *Free and Independent States*; That they are Absolved from all Allegiance to the British Crown, and that all political connection between them and the State of Great Britain, is and ought to be totally dissolved....

This document has inspired revolutionary and national liberation movements throughout the world, even up to the present.

A8.   Statue of Nathan Hale

Nathan Hale, assuming the disguise of a schoolmaster, went among the British on Long Island to gather intelligence about a suspected invasion of New York City. He was apprehended almost immediately, thus failing in his mission. When he refused to become a turncoat, he was condemned to death without benefit of trial and hanged on September 22, 1776, at the age of 21.

Just opposite the statue, at the corner of Broadway and Murray Street, is the site of Montagne's Tavern, the first headquarters of the Sons of Liberty.

A9.   Plaque to Jane Addams

This pioneer social worker cofounded Hull House in Chicago, the first settlement house in the United States (see Lower East Side A6). She was also among those responsible for the organization of the Women's International League for Peace and Freedom and received the Nobel Peace Prize in 1931.

A10.   **Old New York City Courthouse** *a/k/a Criminal Court of the*
City of New York
a/k/a Tweed Ring Courthouse

> This courthouse was built by Boss Tweed;
> Its cost outlay grew like a weed.
> Not a penny was missed—
> They all stuck to his fist;
> Reaching ten million bucks with great speed.
>
> *—Glickman*

In the nineteenth century Tammany Hall was the most powerful Democratic club in the city. It was run by a succession of ward-heelers, the most notorious of whom was William Marcy Tweed, who became Grand Sachem in 1868. Employing a combination of patronage, graft, and outright theft, the Tammany Tigers contrived to turn the entire city of New York into a private endowment. This courthouse went into construction in 1863, budgeted at $250,000. Nine years later it had cost nearly $13 million and was still unfinished. It stands as a monument to the principle that crime doesn't pay unless you think big.

A11.   **Statue of Horace Greeley**
From 1841 to 1872, Horace Greeley was editor and publisher of the *New York Tribune*, one of the most influential papers of the time (see Financial District C7). He took a progressive stand on many issues, denouncing slavery and calling for justice for the foreign-born. In 1844 he took the unprecedented step of hiring Margaret Fuller as a reporter and correspondent. Before then no woman had written for a major newspaper.

TOUR B   *Clerks, Courts, and Cops*

Subway information

Start: Brooklyn Bridge Station (IRT)
#4, #5, or #6 train
Finish: Canal Street Station (IRT)
#6 train

B1.   **Surrogates Court/Hall of Records** *(31 Chambers Street)*
The architecture of this building is a manifestation of the grandiose self-image of New York City at the turn of the century. In 1898 the victory over Spain marked the coming of age of U.S. imperialism. In the same year, Manhattan, the Bronx, Staten Island, Queens, and the former city of Brooklyn consolidated to form the City of New York. The emergence of

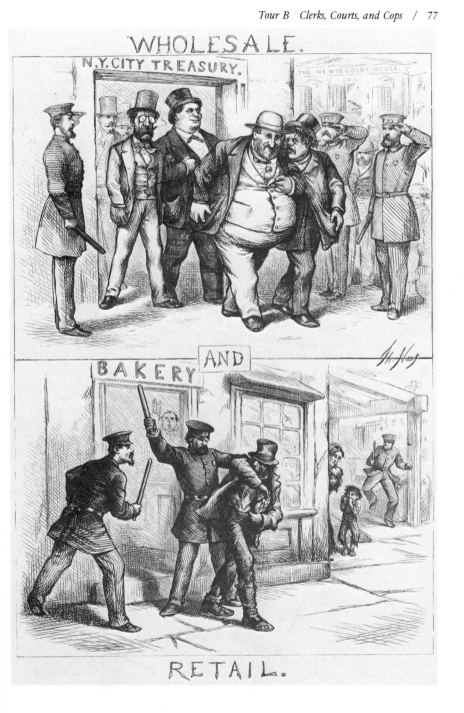

Cartoon by Nast

this new imperial city required edifices commensurate with its status, and in 1899 construction was begun on this building. It is massive in scale and replete with arches, balconies, wood paneling, brass fixtures, and wrought-iron ornamentation.

B2.   Municipal Building *(Chambers Street at Centre Street)*

The Municipal Building, begun as the Hall of Records was being completed, continued the concept of grandeur in public structures. It stands astride the extension of Chambers Street, and in the early days both pedestrians and vehicles passed through its Roman triumphal arch. Because of its massive size, the Municipal Building is often mistaken, even by native New Yorkers, for City Hall. Many city government offices are housed here. Passing through the arch, you emerge into Police Plaza.

B3.   Rhinelander Sugar House Monument *(Police Plaza)*

On the south side of the plaza is a monument enclosing a window from the Rhinelander Sugar House. Like the Livingston Sugar House (see Financial

Courtesy of the Center for Research on Criminal Justice

District D3), this processing plant was converted by the British into a prison during the Revolutionary War.

B4.   Police Headquarters *(Police Plaza)*

This is a very pleasant building. The sand-colored bricks and the plaza and terraces give it a relaxed tone that some other city architects would have done well to emulate. There is a policeman at the door to check your bona fides and a curious sign on the men's room door that warns you to unload firearms on pain of losing your license. (Evidently ladies don't pack rods.) A tour of the building is given daily at 10:30 A.M. and 1:00 P.M. (Call 374-5320 for information.)

Originally, the police force was a motley collection of night watchmen, guards, and marshalls. The latter were paid a bounty for each arrest. The abuses resulting from this caused a public scandal, which forced the city in 1845 to regularize the department. Only 12 years later corruption had become so widespread that a second force was authorized to replace the first, precipitating a riot at City Hall (see Civic Center/Lower West Side A3).

Since its establishment, New York's Finest have been impaled on the horns of the class war. The poor and minorities call for fairness and compassion—often impossible for the police to achieve while they are protecting property and power. The upper echelon demands law and order, which often can be maintained only through repression of the powerless and the radicals. And on top of all this, the police corruption scandals that erupt periodically reveal that the crimefighters themselves can become criminals. (For more on the police, see Civic Center/Lower West Side D7.)

B5.   St. Andrew's Church, Roman Catholic *(St. Andrew's Plaza)*

This building is something of an anomaly: a piece of church property entirely surrounded by government buildings. The original church, consecrated in 1842, stood on the site of what is now the U.S. Courthouse, and served the Irish immigrants of Five Points district (see Lower East Side C3). It was there that the plan for parochial school education in New York was developed. When the newspaper industry took over the Park Row area, the church instituted a "printer's mass" at 2:30 A.M. It now serves the Catholic workers in the Civic Center complex. A historical outline available at the church implies that it has been a champion of the poor and the working class, but the careful reader finds little evidence in the outline to support this.

Just across St. Andrew's Plaza, at what would be the corner of Duane and William Streets, stood the Newsboy's Lodging House. The terrible conditions in Five Points had prompted the founding of the Children's Aid

Society in 1853. The Lodging House, its first project, provided quarters for some of the thousands of homeless boys who had been sleeping in the streets. It operated on a strictly business basis, the children paying for their rooms from the pennies they earned or stole.

During the warm months, the Plaza is transformed into an outdoor cafe. Several good food shops have set up concessions where you can buy sandwiches, seafood, Italian dishes, pastry, and coffee and take them to nearby tables.

B6.   United States Courthouse *(Foley Square)*
In 1949 Room 110 of this building was the scene of the first of a dozen trials of the top leadership of the Communist Party. They were accused of "conspiring to organize a political party which would teach and advocate the duty and necessity of the violent overthrow and destruction of the United States government."

At one point in the trial, a prosecution witness described a spurious plan in which the Soviet army would invade the United States via Alaska and Canada. When the defendants smiled in disbelief, Judge Medina rebuked them. John Gates, editor of the *Daily Worker* and one of the defendants, asked whether, having put them on trial for thinking, the bench was now about to challenge their right to smile. When they were convicted, Medina imposed the maximum sentence: five years. As the coup de grâce, he sentenced the CP lawyers to jail for contempt of court.

In the spring of 1953 the HUAC traveling circus came to town. Thousands of subpoenas were issued and the hearings went on for months. Perhaps the highlight of the event was the performance of a musical setting of the First Amendment. The singer was Jay Gorney, composer of "Brother, Can You Spare a Dime?," a popular song during the 1930s. When he was interrupted by HUAC Chairman Velde, Gorney asserted that since the committee had listened to the "singing" of stool pigeons, it owed him equal time. Velde was not amused.

The deployment of forces in the lobby of the courthouse reflects the edginess with which the federal government eyes its citizenry. There are signs informing us that we are being photographed and that our packages are subject to inspection. A metal detector lies in wait for special cases. Two policemen officiate at the front desk and an armed guard defends the elevators, ever alert for the skulking lurker who harbors a yen for force and violence.

B7.   New York County Courthouse *(Foley Square)*
This was built to replace the Tweed "golden goose" (see Civic Center/ Lower West Side A10). Though similar to the federal courthouse in the columned massiveness of its facade, its interior is much more accessible— no cameras, security guards, or warnings.

"It's Okay—We're Hunting Communists"

– – – – from Herblock Special Report (W.W. Norton & Co., 1974)

Reprinted by permission.

In several parts of the building there are fine examples of WPA murals. Note, for example, the painting on the dome of the huge main rotunda, a historical panorama entitled *Law Through the Ages*. Upstairs, in Rooms 448 and 452, are murals and paintings related to New York history. The murals, newly restored to their original bright colors, are examples of what might be gained by restoration of the many WPA projects elsewhere in the city.

B8. **Thomas Paine Park** *(Foley Square)*
This quiet spot, surrounded by official buildings, is a good place to meditate upon the career of the fiery revolutionary pamphleteer for whom it is named.

Tom Paine was instrumental in mobilizing American public opinion in favor of separation from Britain. On January 9, 1776, six months before the Declaration of Independence was issued, he published *Common Sense*. Within three months it had sold 120,000 copies. Paine wrote:

> Though I would carefully avoid giving unnecessary offence, yet I am inclined to believe, that all those who espouse the doctrine of reconciliation, may be included within the following descriptions. Interested men, who are not to be trusted; weak men, who *cannot* see; prejudiced men, who *will not* see; and a certain set of moderate men, who think better of the European world than it deserves; and this last class, by an ill-judged deliberation, will be the cause of more calamities to this continent, than all the other three.

John Adams, our second president and no particular fan of Paine's, said in 1806: "I know not whether any man in the world has had more influence on its inhabitants or affairs for the last thirty years than Thomas Paine."

Here are some other pungent excerpts from his writings:

> Man has no property in man; neither has any generation a property in the generations which are to follow.
>
> *The Rights of Man (1792)*

> All national institutions of churches, whether Jewish, Christian or Turkish, appear to me no other than human inventions, set up to terrify and enslave mankind, and monopolize power and profit.
>
> *The Age of Reason (1807)*

(For more on Paine, see Greenwich Village A1.)

B9. **Baxter Street** *(near Leonard Street)*
The government buildings in this area are so large and overbearing that it is hard to remember that just around the corner are Chinatown and Little Italy. Before the courts and offices were constructed, the tenements extended much farther west than they do now.

Beginning in 1786, the New York African Society held secret meetings in a house at 42 Baxter Street, later expanding to include 46 Baxter Street. When the buildings were demolished, a trapdoor to a hidden basement was discovered, demonstrating that there was an underground railroad stop here.

In 1847 the Society for the Promotion of Education Among Colored Children was established. It set up a number of schools around the city, one of which—Grammar School Number 4—was in this neighborhood, somewhere on Centre Street.

B10.   **Criminal Courts Building/Manhattan House of Detention**
(100–110 Centre St.)

The huge Criminal Courts Building is decorated with many noble-sounding quotations on the subject of justice. They must provoke bitter irony in the minds of some who pass through these doors:

Only the just man enjoys peace of mind.
Be just and fear not.
Why should there not be a patient confidence in the ultimate justice of
    the people?
Every place is safe to him who lives in justice.

Connected to the courthouse is the prison known as The Tombs. Originally the label was attached to a building here that looked like an Egyptian tomb; more recently it referred to the realities of prison life.

In 1970 conditions inside The Tombs were so bad that an Inmate Liberation Front was organized. In August and again in October the prison was shaken by rebellion. At one point almost a thousand prisoners held several of the guards hostage. The prisoners broke through a two-inch-thick glass block and tossed a message to the street below that said: "We want to be treated like human beings. There is no medication for the sick. Unhealthy cells, unhealthy food. Three men in cells built for one." They revealed that nearly 2,000 men were being held in a facility designed to hold 835. They had been subjected to brutality and some women visitors had been harassed. Many prisoners had been there for more than eight months awaiting trial dates only because they could not raise bail. The Tombs closed in 1974. (For more on this, see Greenwich Village A10.)*

If you look west across Centre Street you will see a huge, black, marble-faced cube that appears to have large chunks clawed out of it. This is the Family Court Building, which also houses the Department of Probation. It is hard to imagine what was going on in the minds of the architects when they designed this bleak, forbidding exterior to house services that should be among the most sensitive to human feelings.

---

*The city is now proposing to reopen the prison, a move violently opposed by the local citizenry.

Courtesy of "For the People"/LNS

TOUR C   Church of Rebellion/Cathedral of Commerce

Subway information

Start and finish: City Hall Station
(BMT) N or RR train

C1.   **The Woolworth Building** *(233 Broadway, between Barclay Street and Park Place)*

In the beginning Frank created the five and the ten. And Frank blessed them saying, Be fruitful and multiply. And these are the generations of the nickel. The nickel begat the dime and the dime begat the quarter and the quarter begat the dollar. And Frank saw the cash, that it was good.

And Frank said, Let the bucks be gathered together unto one place, and let a temple be built. And let it be the tallest on the face of the earth. And let its lobby be fashioned like a cross. And let it bear my likeness and those of my servants upon its arches, and my sign upon its mailbox.

And it came to pass in the nineteen-hundredth and thirteenth year that it was finished. And the Princes of Profit came from near and far to trade within the Cathedral of Commerce. And Frank rested. Amen.

You can see it all today, just as it was then. Ask the guard for the free descriptive leaflet.

C2.   **17 Murray Street** *(between Broadway and Church Street)*

This building houses several progressive organizations. On the fourth floor is the Mutual Aid Project, a training and support center for community organizing and development of local leadership, especially involving older people. On the floor above is a suite shared by the Health Policy Advisory Center (Health/PAC) and the Nurses' Network. Health/PAC puts out a bimonthly bulletin and a growing list of books and pamphlets. Some titles are *The Political Economy of Health* and *American Health Empire: Power, Profits and Politics*. The Nurses' Network began as a spinoff from Health/PAC but is rapidly finding its own path. It publishes a monthly newsletter

THE MASSES   17

Nearer. My God To Thee

Cartoon by Art Young

for nurses and health-care workers, focusing attention on such issues as racism in nursing.

At the end of the Revolutionary War, November 25, 1783 was designated Evacuation Day. On that day the last of the British occupiers were to leave New York. A certain Mrs. Day raised an American flag in her front yard on what is now Murray Street. Major Cunningham, the most hated British officer in the city, took it into his head to remove the flag. Mrs. Day chased Major Cunningham down the entire length of the street, and when she caught up with him, she beat him with her broomstick.

C3.   Church Street *(north and south side of Chambers Street)*
These two sites are important locations in the history of Blacks in New York. In 1827, the year of the emancipation of slaves in New York state, the first Black newspaper ever published in the United States began printing at 150 Church Street. Published by John Russworm and Samuel Cornish, it was called *Freedom's Journal* and it provided a forum for radical black intellectuals.

Across the street, at 156 Church Street, stood the Mother African Methodist Episcopal Zion Church, the first Black church in New York. In 1796 the Black members of the John Street Methodist Church, rebelling against its restrictive and discriminatory practices, broke away under the leadership of James Varick (see Civic Center/Lower West Side D5) and founded a new church in a stable on this site.

The stable was replaced first by a frame building, then one of stone, and finally, in 1840, by one of brick.

In 1829 Sojourner Truth, the escaped slave who became a fiery abolitionist orator, renounced her slave name in the pulpit of this church. She christened herself with these words: "Sojourner, because I am a wanderer; Truth because God is Truth; so Truth shall be my abiding name until I die."

On October 1, 1850, the church was the scene of a mass meeting in support of James Hamlet, a free Black who had been captured in New York under the terms of the Fugitive Slave Law (see Financial District B2). Five hundred dollars was raised to "ransom" him. A delegation of white men went to Baltimore where Hamlet was being held prisoner, paid the money, and brought him home. Subsequently, members of the church formed a vigilance committee whose aim was to prevent others from being abducted into slavery.

Just north of the church was a Black cemetery. Because of prevailing white attitudes, all burials here were required to take place after dark.

C4.   164 Duane Street *(near Hudson Street)*
This building housed the offices and presses of *PM*, a newspaper that

began publication in 1940 with a unique journalistic philosophy. It did not accept advertising of any kind, even from its supporters and friends, and it offered a progressive, populist orientation in an easy-to-read tabloid format. Its editor, Ralph Ingersoll, wrote: "We are against people who push other people around, just for the fun of it, whether they flourish in this country or abroad. We are against fraud and deceit and cruelty and greed, and will seek to expose their practitioners." Marshall Field, its publisher, put it this way: "*PM* has not considered its function to be that of viewing with equal impartiality both sides of the struggles between the strong and the weak, the big and the small, the monopolists and the independents, the intrenched and those who still have their way to make."

PM folded in 1948. Two attempts were made to revive its spirit: first the *New York Star*, then the *Daily Compass*. But cold war politics and newspaper economics proved too tough to overcome. The *Compass* closed in 1952.

The crusading liberal spirit of these newspapers was continued in *I.F. Stone's Weekly*, which was written, edited, produced, and distributed from Izzy and Esther Stone's Washington living room for almost two decades, through the cold war and McCarthyism and well into the turbulent 1960s. Stone, who worked on *PM* and its successors, still writes an occasional column for the liberal press.

C5.   **The American Telephone and Telegraph Company Long Lines Building** *(33 Thomas Street, between Church Street and Broadway)*
This frightful, blind, massive skyscraper is a computer masquerading as a building. When we asked the security guard how people feel about working in a place without windows, he replied, "They need to take a lot of breaks so they don't go crazy." But, he went on, we shouldn't be too concerned—the building is air-conditioned.

Near this address used to stand Grammar School Number 3, one of the schools set up by the Society for the Promotion of Education among Colored Children (see Civic Center/Lower West Side B9).

C6.   **Broadway and Worth Street**
This was the site of the Broadway Tabernacle, whose congregation moved here from the Chatham Street Chapel (see Lower East Side C4). In the autumn of 1853, five years after their pioneering convention at Seneca Falls, New York, the Women's Rights Movement met here. The meeting was attended by the leading activists in the movement, including Lucretia Mott, Susan B. Anthony, Elizabeth Cady Stanton, and Lucy Stone. Stone set the tone for the meetings by wearing Amelia Bloomer's new liberated dress design. This outrage, plus the women's inflammatory speeches demanding full equality with men, provoked angry demonstrations and, at

Photo by Diane Neumaier

Drawn by Art Young.

YOUNG WIFE: YES, WE'VE BEEN MARRIED ALMOST FIVE YEARS,
AND WE NEVER HAD A DIFFERENCE OF OPINION!
SUFFRAGE LECTURER: WHICH ONE IS THE FOOL?

one point, a free-for-all fistfight in the gallery. The convention was front-page news for days.

C7.   **280 Broadway** *(between Chambers and Reade Streets)*
Here stands the Marble Emporium, built to house A.T. Stewart's huge department store. From 1850 to 1870 this masterpiece of merchandising featured an abundance of imported and domestic goods never before found under one roof. With its white marble facade and 15 plate glass show windows, it was the delight of New York's wealthy set, so distinctive that it did not even need an identifying sign. At the time of the Civil War, Stewart was the richest man in the country.

The building was later occupied by the *New York Sun,* whose name it still bears. At the turn of the century the city's flourishing newspaper business was producing more than a dozen daily papers. However, the economics of journalism caused the shrinking of the field, first through merger and finally failure. In 1952 the *Sun* was bought by the *World-Telegram* (itself the product of a merger) and the whole operation folded in 1966. New Yorkers are now confronted with the choice of the conservative *Times*, the reactionary *News*, and the unspeakable *Post*—the Daily Drab, the Daily Drivel, and the Daily Drool.

TOUR D   SoHo

Subway information

Start: Prince Street Station (BMT)
N or RR train
Finish: Canal Street Station (BMT)
N or RR train

D1.   Spring Street *(off Broadway)*

The spring for which this street is named ran along here, past the estate of Aaron Burr. In June 1799 Burr made a half-hearted gesture toward fulfilling his Manhattan Water Company charter by drilling a well here and laying a few miles of wooden pipe. By September he was pursuing his pet project: drilling a hole in Alexander Hamilton's banking monopoly. (See Financial District B8 for more of the story.)

D2.   New Deal Restaurant *(152 Spring Street, between Wooster Street and West Broadway)*

For an example of how history can be trivialized and exploited, step inside this expensive restaurant and observe the depression-chic atmosphere conjured up by its all-black decor and pseudo-WPA-style murals. The only thing missing is a breadline. Across the street is a bookstore that carries information about the area.

(The next entry is somewhat out of the way, but is worth the walk.)

D3.   New York Feminist Art Institute *(325 Spring Street at Washington Street)*

The institute was founded in 1977 and opened in 1979. Its curriculum combines practical art training and women's studies. Its aim is "to create and to increase self-awareness and to teach the skills necessary for the visual translation of the personal point of view within a historical and political context." Although there is at present no gallery at the institute, you may be able to see works displayed informally in the studios.

Photos by Diane Neumaier

D4. **100 Avenue of the Americas*** *(near Watts and Thompson Streets)*
Over much of the second story of this mysterious building are bas-reliefs
showing workers at their jobs. We have been unable to trace the origin of

---

*This is really Sixth Avenue, and all New Yorkers call it by that name. "Avenue of the
Americas" was tacked on in 1945 when the United States was playing "good neighbor" to the
campesinos and colonels south of the border.

these figures, beyond the fact that the building was acquired by the Trinity Corporation in 1932, when it was decked out with such luxuries as fireplaces in the executive offices. If you know more about this building, please write to us.

D5.   Statue of Juan Pablo Duarte (*between Varick Street and Sixth Avenue, near Canal Street*)

Duarte was the leader of a national liberation struggle on the island of Hispaniola in the mid-nineteenth century. Hispaniola, originally colonized by Spain but eventually ceded to France, retained both French- and

Spanish-speaking areas. In 1803 a revolution led by the great Black
freedom fighter, Toussaint L'Ouverture, achieved independence from
France. The French area, now known as Haiti, came to dominate the
Spanish area, known as Santo Domingo.

Duarte was one of the organizers of a secret society in Santo Domingo
that overthrew Haitian rule and established the independent Dominican
Republic. But the aftermath was a voluntary ceding of this hard-won
independence back to Spain by a military faction opposed to Duarte. He
spent much of his later life in exile in Venezuela.

Varick Street is named for Richard Varick, a Revolutionary patriot.
Varick is also the surname of several important blacks, who may have been

slaves or ex-slaves of the Richard Varick family. Cesar Varick was one of the leaders of the Slave Rebellion of 1741 (see Financial District A7). James Varick was the founder of the AME Zion Church, which played an important role in the antislavery movement (see Civic Center/Lower West Side C3).

D6. Canal Street Post Office *(at Church Street)*
Just inside the main entrance to the post office is a fine example of WPA art. It is a bas-relief, dating from 1938, of a Native American archer in a celestial setting. This beautifully formed figure carries no arrows and a bow without a string, reflecting the romantic notion of the Indian as noble savage. The work is in excellent condition.

D7. 36 Lispenard Street *(corner of Church Street)*
This is the site of the residence of David Ruggles, a Black abolitionist and conductor on the underground railroad. Ruggles aided at least 600 escaped slaves, including Frederick Douglass, whom he sheltered here in 1838. Douglass later became one of the leading abolitionist writers and orators. His commanding presence and profound intellect challenged those who believed in the "natural inferiority" of Blacks.

D8. Old Police Headquarters *(240 Centre Street, between Broome and Grand Streets)*
This ornate and somber building is now closed and quiet, but some 60 years ago it was the scene of one of the most odious incidents of the post-World War I era. The ruling class went into a flap as a result of the Russian Revolution and the worldwide wave of unrest that followed the armistice. To forestall a leftward movement here, it precipitated a series of attacks that became known as the Palmer Raids. On the evening of November 7–8, 1919, some 2,000 "reds" were rounded up and brought to this building. All noncitizens were summarily deported.

A block from police headquarters, on Mulberry Street, just around the corner from Broome Street, a murder was committed on February 10, 1921. The killer, apprehended almost immediately, was a hit man for a Rhode Island mob. Three-and-a-half months later, Nicola Sacco and Bartolomeo Vanzetti went on trial in Massachusetts, accused of killing a guard in Braintree the previous year. It was never brought to the attention of the jury in the Sacco-Vanzetti case that the gun used in the Mulberry Street murder was almost certainly the same weapon that killed the guard in Braintree. The two anarchists were put to death in 1927, still protesting their innocence.

Late in 1929 the old Loft's candy factory across from headquarters was converted into a police college. This institution was designed to improve the cops and make them classy. Some officers were given pay raises and directed to "teach." The men were required to purchase fancy new clothes and were directed to "learn." And learn they did. Four weeks later, person or persons unknown removed everything in the building that wasn't nailed down, compelling the department to install round-the-clock guards and lock the lightbulbs in their sockets.

During the Vietnam War, the outposts of the power structure came under siege from increasingly active urban guerrillas. Bombings of corporations, draft boards, chemical warfare research institutions, and police stations reached a high point during the early 1970s. On June 9, 1970, a member of the Weathermen penetrated this building, getting past a four-man patrol, an I.D. check, and a briefcase search. After signing in, he asked to use the men's room, was personally escorted past the hallway patrol guards, and planted a bomb that blew out one wing of the building several hours later.

"Couple of guys named Marx and Engels. Find 'em and give 'em the works."   NED HILTON

Ned Hilton, International Publishers Co. Inc. Reprinted with permission.

TOUR A

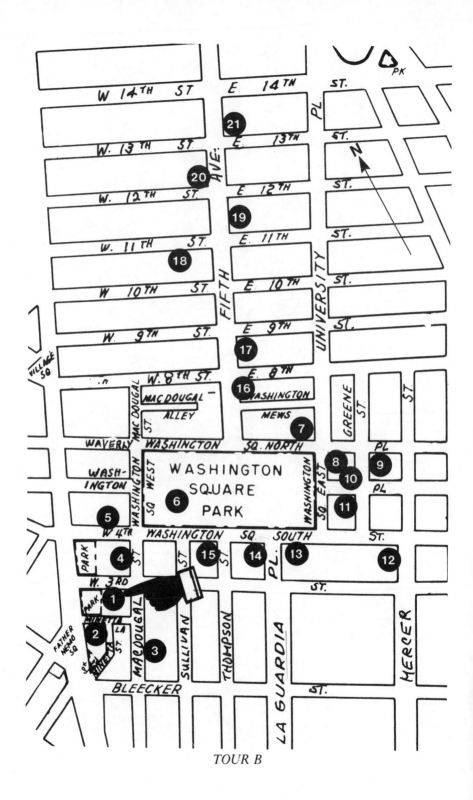

TOUR B

6
Greenwich Village

The ideal of quiet and of genteel retirement, in 1835, was found in Washington Square, where the Doctor built himself a handsome, modern, wide-fronted house, with a big balcony before the drawingroom windows, and a flight of white marble steps ascending to a portal which was also faced with white marble.... In front of them was the square, containing a considerable quantity of inexpensive vegetation, enclosed by a wooden paling, which increased its rural and accessible appearance; and round the corner was the more august precinct of The Fifth Avenue, taking its origin at this point with a spacious and confident air which already marked it for high destinies.

—Henry James
Washington Square

... a world of pace-setters, a whole neighborhood of tolerators, a place where a girl could cut off her hair or excel at chess without every eyebrow in town going up. A place where you could mingle with the beats in the famous cafes of MacDougal Street (San Remo, Gaslight, Rienzi, Figaro, Cafe Passé, Cafe Lucia) while baroque concerti drifted out of speakers and mingled with the rococo curls of tobacco smoke. At last a place where sex was okay and money wasn't everything, where people like Marx, Freud, and Maxwell Bodenheim were precursors of us.

Us! World-shakers of the world!

—Alix Kates Shulman
Burning Questions

The uniqueness of Greenwich Village derives from its physical appearance and the people who live here. The Village is one of the few neighborhoods in Manhattan that has remained relatively unchanged since the early nineteenth century. Its narrow, winding streets and many of its small, handsome houses date from that period. As the city grew around it, the Old World, human-scaled quality of the Village became more rare, and more valued by its residents. In recent years they have had to fight hard to preserve it—with mixed success, as witness the imposition of NYU buildings on the south and east sides of Washington Square.

Greenwich Village began its existence in colonial days as a small town, and until the twentieth century remained relatively isolated from the rest of the city. Seventh Avenue South did not transect the Village until 1910, and it was almost two decades later that Sixth Avenue was extended this far south. In addition, the Village had the benefit of a geological coincidence: the bedrock under the area is too far below ground to make skyscraper construction practicable, and so developers avoided the area.

After the exodus northward of the wealthy, whose forebears had built Greenwich Village in the early nineteenth century, Italian immigrants moved into the area around Bleecker Street, and other parts of the Village became a haven for nonconformists. This latter quality remains one of its special attributes. Since the early days of the twentieth century, Village people have been able to pursue unconventional lifestyles and be not only accepted but respected. Here artists, writers, radicals, and free-thinkers feel comfortable. Greenwich Village is a place where one can walk barefoot without being stared at; where an interracial couple or a homosexual couple can stroll without being gaped at; where one can hand out leaflets and expect people to take them, read them, and talk about them. The Village has come to symbolize a challenge to the American Way of Life.

TOUR A   The West Village

Subway information

Start: Sheridan Square Station (IRT)
#1 train
Finish: 14th Street Station (IRT) #1,
#2, or #3 train

A1.   **Marie's Crisis Cafe** *(59 Grove Street, west of Seventh Avenue)*
This is the site of the house in which Thomas Paine died in 1809. The "Crisis" in its name refers to Paine's great *Crisis Papers*, which he published beginning in the winter of 1776–77 to restore the flagging spirits of the people. The *Papers* begin:

> These are the times that try men's souls: The summer soldier and the sunshine patriot will, in this crisis, shrink from the service of his country; but he that stands it NOW, deserves the love and thanks of man and woman. Tyranny, like hell, is not easily conquered; yet we have this

consolation with us, the harder the conflict, the more glorious the triumph. What we obtain too cheap, we esteem too lightly: 'Tis dearness only that gives every thing its value. Heaven knows how to put a proper price upon its goods; and it would be strange indeed, if so celestial an article as FREEDOM should not be highly rated.

In 1787 Paine left for Europe, where he played a minor role in the French Revolution. When he returned to the United States 15 years later, he was received coldly. The Americans were antagonistic to the excesses of the French Revolution, with which he was identified, and they condemned him as an atheist as well. A scant 30 years after he had galvanized the country with the *Crisis Papers*, he died here, destitute and stripped of the U. S. citizenship he had been awarded.

A plaque on the side of the cafe pays tribute to the international scope of Paine's influence. (For more on Paine, see Civic Center/Lower West Side B8.)

A2.   Theater de Lys *(121 Christopher Street, near Bedford Street)*

In the 1950s small-theater activity in Greenwich Village increased enormously, and a new term was coined: "Off-Broadway." These theaters had in common small size and shoestring budgets. Their low ticket prices made possible the development of new audiences among students and the less affluent; their unconventional theater design and small size established an intimacy between audience and players. Minimal financial investment encouraged inventiveness in production techniques and allowed companies to take chances on new plays, unknown playwrights, and untried casts.

Some of this avant-garde theater was politically controversial as well. Theater de Lys, along with Cherry Lane (see Greenwich Village A5) and Circle-in-the Square, to name but a few, produced new or seldom-seen plays by such writers as Sean O'Casey, Alice Childress, Arthur Miller, and Barbara Garson. Theater de Lys housed the history-making seven-year run of the Brecht-Weill *Threepenny Opera*.

Many Off-Broadway theaters continue to operate in the Village. The new avant-garde is called Off-Off-Broadway, and may be found in lofts, theaters, and converted garages throughout the city. The best source of performance listings is the *Village Voice*.

A3.   102 Bedford Street *(near Grove Street)*

Here stands what is surely one of the most extraordinary houses in New York. It is a tiny cottage, two diminutive stories high. It looks like a freshly painted sharecropper's shack and, indeed, the house is believed to have been used as slave quarters in the eighteenth century.

Photo by Diane Neumaier

A4.   **West Village Houses** *(west side of Washington Street, from Morton to Christopher Streets and from West 10 to Bank Streets)*

These houses are the spoils of victory for a band of Davids who fought and conquered the Big City Goliath. There were to have been high-rise apartments here, but the people of the neighborhood organized to defeat the plan, substituting one for five- and six-story buildings. These were erected in 1974.

One of the leaders of the fight was Jane Jacobs, a long-time activist, analyst of the dynamics of urban life, and passionate advocate of humanistic city planning. Her pioneering book, *The Death and Life of Great American Cities*, is based largely upon her experiences in New York.

A5.   **Cherry Lane Theater** *(38 Commerce Street, near Bedford Street)*

In the 1920s the New Playwrights Theater was based here. It featured the early efforts of Michael Gold, John Dos Passos, and John Howard Lawson. Gold later became an important cultural figure in the Communist Party; Dos Passos wrote several radical novels and then grew more and more conservative; Lawson moved to Hollywood and worked as a screenwriter. After World War II, he was one of a group hauled before HUAC in the first postwar anti-Red purges. He and some of the others of the Hollywood Ten spent a year in jail for their invocation of the First Amendment.

In 1951 Julian Beck and Judith Malina founded the anarchist Living Theater at Cherry Lane, only to be hounded out of the building within a year for allegedly violating fire regulations. But their pursuers did not let up; Beck and Malina were finally forced to flee the country to escape harassment from the Internal Revenue Service.

Commerce Street seems like a singularly inappropriate name for this quiet residential lane; in fact, it was originally Cherry Lane. When in 1822 New York was in the grip of one of its periodic yellow fever epidemics, many of those who could afford to left the city in hopes of escaping contamination. They moved to Greenwich Village and set up their commercial establishments here, eventually changing the name of the street. Bank Street, a few blocks north, had a similar origin.

A6.   **Greenwich House** *(27 Barrow Street, east of Seventh Avenue)*

The Greenwich House Settlement was founded in 1902 and moved here in 1917. One of its first services was a child-care program for working mothers, and one of its first concerns was the health and welfare of its constituents, in aid of which it lobbied vigorously for improved sanitation and for control of child labor. Later its services expanded to include health care, recreational and sports programs, evening classes, and a theater program. A wonderful photo in one of its brochures, taken in the 1920s, shows a group of serious-faced children and their health-care instructor standing at attention, toothbrushes at the ready, beside a sign advertising a free dental clinic.

Greenwich House now operates programs at eight locations; its music school and pottery offer instruction to neighborhood residents at low cost. (For more on settlement houses, see Lower East Side A6.)

Barrow Street is named for an artist who drew a picture of Trinity Church. It was previously called Reason Street, after Thomas Paine's famous anticlerical work, *The Age of Reason*. The street name was changed at the request of Trinity. (For more Trinity tricks, see Financial District B13.)

A7.   92 Grove Street *(just west of Waverly Place)*

In 1863, in the midst of the Civil War, sagging enlistments and a series of defeats had depleted the Union forces to such a point that a draft was initiated. Many working-class whites were furious at having to fight to free Blacks whom they saw as competitors, and outraged at the policy that allowed the rich to buy their way out of service. They precipitated a series of bloody riots in the city, which created a state of anarchy that lasted several days, leaving in their wake $5 million in property damage and more than 400 people, mostly Black, dead or injured. During the Draft Riots the occupants of this house sheltered a number of Blacks, hiding them in the basement until it was safe to emerge.

A8.   51 Christopher Street *(east of Seventh Avenue)*

This is now a restaurant called "Bagel and ...." In 1969 it was the Stonewall Inn, one of several gay bars in the Village. The police were in the habit of harassing the customers of these bars, but on the night of June 28, the victims fought back.

The cops, armed with a warrant, entered the Stonewall Inn at about 3 A.M. and, using the ploy that the bar was dispensing liquor without a license, they evicted all 200 customers. Within a few minutes the 200 had surrounded the police inside and were bombarding them with everything throwable. The siege lasted for about 45 minutes, by which time the attackers had doubled in number. Several police were injured and 13 gays were arrested.

The next night another battle erupted, lasting twice as long. The cops were unable to handle the situation and sent for the tactical police force. These helmeted honchos linked arms and swept back and forth along Christopher Street, trying to disperse the gays, who would slip into side streets, regroup, and return in back of the police lines.

The Stonewall Riots were a turning point in the evolution of gay consciousness—from passive acceptance of harassment to militant re-

Courtesy of Peg Averill/LNS

sistance—and marked the birth of the Gay Rights Movement. The annual Gay Pride March, which takes place on the anniversary of the riot, is one of the manifestations of the movement's new pride and solidarity.

A9.   **Northern Dispensary** *(Waverly Place and Christopher Street)*
In 1790 the New York State Medical Society recommended that New York City establish a dispensary "for the medical relief of the sick poor of the city." The first such dispensary was opened near where City Hall now stands. The Northern Dispensary, so named because it was at the northern boundary of the city, was the second to be built. It has been in continuous service here since 1827.

A10.   **Jefferson Market Library** *(425 Sixth Avenue, at*
                                          Greenwich Avenue)
This century-old landmark, which was formerly a courthouse and part of a complex including a jail and a market, was slated to be torn down in 1967. Neighborhood resistance forced cancellation of the demolition and the building was converted into a branch of the New York Public Library. The interior is as extravagant and fanciful as the exterior, with arches, curved

staircases, and intricate stonework now partially concealed by book-shelves.

Adjacent to the library is a beautiful, well-tended community garden. Until 1974 the site was desecrated by the infamous Women's House of Detention. Dorothy Day (see East Village B5) was incarcerated there in 1957 for civil disobedience. She wrote:

> We four political prisoners had cells next to each other. We were two in a cell, on the most airless corridor, with the darkest cubicles. We had a dim, twenty-five-watt bulb in ours, Judith Beck and I, until the last week of our thirty days, when a tall, young colored woman brought us a fifty-watt bulb from a neighboring cell just vacated. . . . [F]rom the time one is arrested until the time one leaves a prison, every event seems calculated to intimidate and to render uncomfortable and ugly the life of the prisoner.*

Sometimes the sense of community triumphed over these harsh conditions. In 1970, when a citizens' committee was organized to secure bail for women awaiting trial, the prisoners decided that the best way to choose who would receive the bail money was by vote. By common agreement they decided that those freed would work with the committee to raise funds for other incarcerated women.

Perhaps the most famous inmate of the House of D. was Angela Davis. She was picked up on October 13, 1970, for extradition to California where she was wanted on charges of murder, kidnapping, and conspiracy in connection with an attempt to free the Soledad Brothers, Black men who were being held in prison in California. Inside the prison, she went on a hunger strike to protest being kept in isolation, and succeeded in being transferred to a regular cell. Outside, on Greenwich Avenue, there were continuous demonstrations demanding freedom for political prisoners and an end to racism.

At 3 A.M. on December 22, Davis was taken from her cell, handcuffed, hustled into a waiting police van, and driven in a nine-car convoy to The Tombs. There she was handed over to California authorities, transferred to another car, and sped through the darkened city to the Holland Tunnel, which had been cleared of cars in both directions; nothing must prevent the delivery of one of the F.B.I.'s most wanted fugitives. From New Jersey she was flown back to California, put on trial, and in the end exonerated.

The growing politicization of prisoners was becoming a threat to the authorities. Protests and demonstrations were taking place inside and

---

*Dorothy Day, *Loaves and Fishes* (New York: Curtis Books, n.d.).

outside both the Women's House of Detention and The Tombs. In 1971, Attica burned. With the spectre of more of the same before them, the authorities acted. In 1974 all prisoners were relocated to Rikers Island, rendering them invisible and inaccessible.

A11.   **Patchin Place** *(off West 10 Street, near Sixth Avenue)* and **Milligan Place** *(off Sixth Avenue, between West 10 and West 11 Streets)*
These streets are small, unexpected pockets of serenity. The houses on them were built in the middle of the nineteenth century to board waiters who worked at the now-defunct Hotel Brevoort on Fifth Avenue. Early in the twentieth century, they served as residences for many writers.

John Reed was one of those writers. In the short space of three years, he made a dramatic transition from Harvard playboy to successful reporter to revolutionary writer and fighter for justice. During this time he lived in Greenwich Village, first at 42 Washington Place and then here, at 1 Patchin Place. It was while living here that he wrote one of the finest books on the Russian Revolution: *Ten Days that Shook the World*. He died of typhus in the Soviet Union in 1920 and is buried in the Kremlin Wall in Moscow.

At about the same time, Jim Larkin lived in a meager room in Milligan Place. This Irish revolutionary was, like Reed, one of the founders of the CPUSA. For this offense he was imprisoned in Sing Sing until 1923, and then deported.

A12.   **South Side of West 11 Street, Just East of Sixth Avenue**
On the fence in front of this tiny triangle of ground is a plaque that reads: "The Second Cemetery of the Spanish and Portuguese Synagogue Shearith Israel in the City of New York 1805–1829." The cemetery was destroyed and the remains moved north for reburial when the city street grid was laid out. Compare this treatment of "hallowed ground" with the immunity granted Henry Brevoort's orchard further east on this same street (see East Village A8).

A13.   **The New School** *(66 West 12 Street, between Fifth and Sixth Avenues)*
This building houses the undergraduate and adult divisions of the New School (see Greenwich Village B21). When it was erected in 1929, the school's president, Alvin Johnson, commissioned two murals for its public rooms. Despite the great fame of their artists—Thomas Hart Benton, a leading American Realist, and José Orozco, the great Mexican artist—the paintings were rarely seen by anyone outside the school community. Each of them has in its own way suffered the fate of proletarian art in this country. The Orozco is unpublicized and uncared for, fading and flaking while the school has been unable to raise funds for its restoration (perhaps

no surprise, since it features a portrait of Vladimir Ilyitch Lenin). The
The Benton has recently been sold and sat in storage in a Manhattan art
gallery, awaiting the favor of a wealthy patron. Once has recently
materialized: Equitable Life has bought it for display in its new corporate
headquarters uptown.

The Orozco is in Room 705. You may have to wait to enter, but it is
well worth the wait. In any case, you will be able to see one of the panels,
which is outside the classroom.

A14. Food and Maritime Trades High School (208 West 13 Street, near Seventh Avenue)

This gloomy, dark-red brick building was erected just after the Civil War. It
is a vocational school attended primarily by working-class kids. In 1968 a
young teacher was suspended for supporting a group of students in their
attempt to form a student court. This court would have created a "jury of
their peers" for those threatened with disciplinary action. As the end of the
school year approached, the angry students, with a little help from their
friends from other high schools, walked out and picketed the building.
Although the incident was brief, it was significant in that it reflected the
enlargement of student protest beyond the universities into the high
schools, and beyond the middle class into the working class.

The strange white building between the school and Seventh Avenue
used to house the offices of the National Maritime Union, which explains
its portholes. The NMU, which represents the crews of merchant ships, was
a progressive union in the 1930s and 1940s, but it caved in to McCarthyism
in the 1950s.

A15. Gansevoort Dock (Gansevoort Street at the Hudson River)

This lonely and isolated spot was once a main depot for the great clipper
ship trade of the nineteenth century. From 1866 to 1885, a man worked
here at the humdrum job of customs inspector, a man who only long after
his death came to be recognized as one of our greatest authors: Herman
Melville. After publishing a series of works of increasing profundity that
met with increasing critical rejection, Melville spent what could have been
19 of his most fruitful years checking invoices.

In 1900, nine years after Melville's death, Barret Wendell, the
respected Harvard literary critic, dismissed him in one sentence:

> Herman Melville, with his books about the South Seas, which Robert
> Louis Stevenson is said to have declared the best ever written, and with
> his novels of maritime adventure, began a career of literary promise,
> which never came to fruition.

TOUR B   Washington Square/Lower Fifth Avenue

Subway information

Start: West 4th Street Station (IND)
Finish: West 14th Street Station
(IND) F or BB train

B1.   Gerde's Folk City *(130 West 3 Street, east of Sixth Avenue)*
This is one of the oldest folk music clubs in the city, a mecca during the folk revival of the 1960s. On the wall outside are photos of Bob Dylan and Judy Collins, taken when they made their New York debuts here in 1961. Folk City still holds one night a week open for unknowns to sing before a live audience.

B2.   Minetta Lane *(between Sixth Avenue and MacDougal Street)*
Minetta Lane and Minetta Street, which meets it, were named for the brook that flowed past here. A group of freed Black slaves came to this spot in 1640 to set up the first independent Black enclave in what is now New York City.

B3.   110 MacDougal Street *(near Minetta Lane)*
In 1957 Israel Young opened a small store here, which soon became a center of the folk revival. The Folklore Center was the place to go for books, records, banjo picks, and guitar strings, as well as information on who was singing where and when. There were concerts and poetry readings here, and at almost any time you dropped in, someone was picking and strumming. During the 1961 Folk Song Riots (see Greenwich Village B6), Young was the spokesperson for the folkniks, instituting a lawsuit that reached the state supreme court before the singers won the right to meet in Washington Square Park, making the suit moot. Young now runs a folklore center in Stockholm; New York's Folklore Center is at 321 Sixth Avenue, near West 3 Street.

MacDougal Street is named after Alexander MacDougal, a member of the Sons of Liberty, who was arrested and imprisoned in 1770 on a charge of seditious libel—the result of a pamphlet he had written attacking British colonial policy. Although he was given the opportunity to be free on bail, he chose to embarrass the British by remaining in prison and receiving "guests" there. Eventually his cell got so crowded that he could see people only by appointment.

B4. **Provincetown Playhouse** *(133 MacDougal Street, between West 3 and West 4 Streets)*

In 1915 an experimental theater opened in Provincetown, Massachusetts. Four years later it moved here and set up permanent residence, quickly becoming one of the country's leading theatrical enterprises. John Reed and Eugene O'Neill were two of its moving spirits. (For more on Reed, see Greenwich Village A11.) O'Neill's play *Emperor Jones* was first produced here in 1920. The title character is a Black man and, in an unprecedented move, the Provincetown Players decided to cast a Black actor in the role, instead of a white actor in blackface. The play opened in New York with Charles Gilpin playing Brutus Jones; when the play moved to London, the part was played by the young Paul Robeson.

Also in this building were Polly's Eatery, the Boni Brothers Bookshop, and the Liberal Club, gathering places for radical bohemians before World War I. They ate and talked at Polly's; they read and talked at the bookstore; and they talked and talked at the Liberal Club. Margaret Sanger lectured on birth control at the Liberal Club, as did Alexander Berkman on anarchism; the Washington Square Players began there, producing one act-plays in a tiny room without scenery, props, or costumes.

Polly's was owned by Paula Holladay. On the eve of the execution of Sacco and Vanzetti in August 1927, she walked from Provincetown to Boston, carrying a sign that read, "Is justice dead? Free Sacco and Vanzetti." The Boni Brothers went on to become publishers of radical books. Other members of this circle (Max Eastman, Crystal Eastman, John Reed, and Art Young) began an important magazine: the *Masses*, whose lineal descendants included the *Liberator*, the *New Masses*, and *Masses and Mainstream*. (For the *Masses* trial, see Civic Center/Lower West Side A5.)

B5. **Washington Square United Methodist Church** *(135 West 4 Street, near Sixth Avenue)*

This church has long been a haven for progressive causes, offering space at low cost for meetings, rallies, and cultural events. Among its current tenants are a day-care center and Mobilization for Survival, an antinuke organization. Inside a small door to the right of the church steps you will find a bulletin board and a literature table full of leaflets and announcements of events of interest to the progressive community.

B6. **Washington Square Park**

This is the hub of Greenwich Village, a nearly-24-hour-a-day circus of activity. During good weather the park is alive with frisbee players, disco roller-skaters, joggers, musicians, and chess buffs. And there is the common but unsettling scene of kids playing among spaced-out druggies nodding in the sun. In the center of the park is a lovely fountain whose water play is subject to the vagaries of the New York City water supply. On the south side is a mosaic set into a raised concrete plaza, one of the Cityarts community projects. Near it stands an unexceptional statue of the Italian revolutionary, Garibaldi, bearing the curious stenciled legend "Banned in Chicago; Returned to New York." The presence of his statue here reflects the fact that there is a sizable Italian population in the southern part of the Village, especially in the neighborhood of Bleecker Street.

The city acquired this land in 1797 for use as a potter's field and hanging ground. Victims of destitution and the hangman's noose were buried side by side in unmarked graves. The wealthy, who began to move into the neighborhood during the 1820s, found these sordid goings-on distasteful, and arranged for the area to be fenced in. It re-emerged in 1828 as a parade ground and a strolling place for New York's leading citizens.

In 1889, on the centennial of Washington's inauguration, a wooden triumphal arch was built across Fifth Avenue, a block north of the park. Three years later a committee led by William Rhinelander Stewart of nearby 17 Washington Square North (no doubt with his eye on land values) raised funds to have a permanent arch erected at its present site. This was one of the last gestures of the rich in the area; they soon began their exodus to the green pastures and golden climes bordering Central Park.

In the twentieth century, the community has come to use the park as a vast stage. One evening in 1916, a band of Liberal Club zanies, fortified with revolutionary ardor and enhanced by midwinter madness, climbed to the top of the Washington Arch. Sustained by hot water bottles for the posterior and jugs of wine for the interior, armed with cap pistols, Japanese lanterns, and red balloons, they proclaimed the establishment of the "Independent Republic of Greenwich Village." When the water cooled and the jugs were empty, they descended. This appears to have been the sole foray of the Greenwich Village Liberation Army.

The Great Depression was as catastrophic for the artists living in the Village as for other working people. Not only was there a shortage of patrons (many of whom were joining the artists on the breadlines), but other sources of income had dried up as well. In 1932, impoverished and desperate, 500 of them petitioned the parks commissioner for permission to set up an art show in Washington Square Park, "asking nothing more than is granted puschcart peddlers." The commissioner, viewing with distaste the prospect of this horde of paint-spattered eccentrics descending on his park, denied the request. Only after a great public outcry did he change his mind. And so was born the Washington Square Art Show, which over 50 years later is still attracting tourists to Greenwich Village.

That Washington Square Park is today a people's park is due largely to the fighting spirit of the citizens of Greenwich Village. In 1957 the City

Planning Commission came up with the droll idea that New York traffic needed a right-of-way through Washington Square, and approved a plan for a two-lane road through its heart. New York University administrators loved the idea; Robert Moses, the city's Master Builder, objected: too narrow—only four lanes would do.

The community's response was immediate and violent. Not only did it resolve to fight the road, but it would see to it that *all* traffic was barred from the park, including the buses that had been using it as a turnaround. An alphabet soup of citizens' groups mobilized. Rallies were held and petitions signed. Eleanor Roosevelt and some of her fellow residents wrote a letter to the *Times* accusing the commission of trying to create fancy new addresses by inventing a "South Fifth Avenue." It took seven years of dogged persistence, but the community won, and celebrated with a big party in the park on September 3, 1963.

The folk song revival, which came to full flower in the 1960s, had its inception two or three decades earlier when the progressive movement came to realize that workers create culture as well as commodities. By the late 1940s, young people, attracted by the music, the ambience, and, increasingly, the politics, were coming in greater and greater numbers to participate in informal Sunday afternoon sings around the fountain in Washington Square Park.

In 1961, in the midst of the turmoil over "South Fifth Avenue," Parks Commissioner Newbold Morris took it into his head that "things were getting out of hand," and banned the folkniks from the park. But instead of packing up their picks and going home, they resisted. On Sunday, April 9, there was a two-hour riot: hundreds fought the police. Ten were arrested and 50 others took sanctuary in Judson Memorial Church (see Greenwich Village B15). The next Sunday there was a rally of 500 at the church. A week later the number of demonstrators reached 2,000; one carried a sign reading, "Folk Singing Now—Chess Players Next and Then the Sparrows." The following Sunday there was nearly another riot as one of the thousands present was arrested and manhandled by the cops. The next week, after an adverse ruling by the state supreme court, the folk singers read the law and concluded that it only forbade instruments; so they gathered in the park and sang accompanied only by the men in blue. Finally, fed up with the Fighting Folk, embattled Mayor Robert F. Wagner, Jr., gave in: they could have the park between 3:00 and 6:00 each Sunday if they would play nice. These hootenannies continued throughout the 1960s.

B7.　3 Washington Square North

Most of the buildings north of the park look as they did at the turn of the century, but are no longer the elegant residences they once were, nor the bohemian rooming houses they became later on. Most are now owned by New York University and used for offices.

This building was one such rooming house. During the early 1920s John Dos Passos lived here and wrote *Manhattan Transfer*. Dos Passos, one of a group of writers who had been radicalized by World War I, became one of the mainstays of the literary left in the interwar period. His magnum opus was *USA*, a three-volume blockbuster that incorporated avant-garde writing techniques with progressive politics.

B8.   **100 Washington Square East** *(corner of Waverly Place)*
Constructed around the turn of the century, this is the main building of New York University, the largest private university in the country. NYU was chartered in 1831, when its first governing council was presided over by Albert Gallatin, who had been Secretary of the Treasury from 1801 to 1814. The same year it was chartered, Gallatin became president of the National Bank (later renamed the Gallatin Bank).

The present building replaced the original seat of the university, which had been completed in 1837. The character of the institution was established even before the first stone was laid. Looking to get something for nothing, NYU officials arranged with the governor for Sing Sing Prison to supply free stone from its quarry and convict labor to cut it. In the summer of 1834 the city's stonemasons, incensed at this loss of jobs, demonstrated in Washington Square Park. Troops were sent in and the park became a battleground. Four days later, when the demonstration had been put down, seven workers lay dead. A fragment of the original building stands on a pedestal in Gould Plaza, between Warren Weaver Hall and Bobst Library (see Greenwich Village B12 and B13). It is part of the Founders' Memorial, which of course makes no reference to the circumstances surrounding its construction.

In spite of the bitter opposition of its neighbors in Greenwich Village, NYU has expanded until it now owns at least 80 percent of the property around the square, as well as much of the other real estate in the area. In the process it has secured the collaboration of the City Planning Commission, which has permitted it to tear down many beautiful landmarks and replace them with boxes of largely undistinguished design.

As it grew in size, it also grew in scope. In 1971 a group of students, faculty, and workers at NYU published *NYU INC*. Here is what they say:

> NYU is a giant conglomerate corporation, engaged in a wide range of activities including real estate speculation and development, light manufacturing, investment and speculation in stocks and bonds, communications, retailing, research services on hire to both business and

government, and, finally, the sale of various services such as hospital care and teaching. The Corporation has assets of about $600 million and annual sales of over $200 million. It is owned by a Board of Directors of self-selected millionaires and corporate lawyers and managed by a highly-paid group of top executives.

NYU, Inc. has owned factories for the production of piston rings, cookies, spaghetti, china, envelopes, draperies and shoes. It owns and operates a stone quarry, luxury and slum apartment buildings, hotels, town houses, commercial concert halls, a press, several stores, and a pool of long-term liquid investment capital of over $100 millions. Head-quartered in New York City, it has plants and operations in at least a dozen U.S. cities, Puerto Rico, and several foreign countries.

In the spring of 1968, a recruiter for the Dow Chemical Corporation set up shop in the seventh-floor placement office here. A group representing a coalition of student organizations occupied the office to protest the presence of this producer of napalm. The nervous recruiter was spirited out of the building. NYU officials tried to intimidate the activists by getting the names of the protesters, only to be thwarted when they were presented with a scroll on which hundreds of students identified themselves as participants in the action.

B9.   Kimball Hall *(246 Greene Street, at Waverly Place)*
During the nationwide student strike that took place in the spring of 1970 to protest the U.S. invasion of Cambodia, a group of students and local residents occupied the printing facilities of NYU, which are housed here. They turned the tools to the cause of resistance by using the presses to produce strike literature. The Kimball Collective soon became the citywide center for the printing of leaflets and posters.

B10.   245 Greene Street *(at Washington Place)*
In September 1909 the owners of the Triangle Shirtwaist Company, a factory located on the top three floors of the building then occupying this site, learned that some of their workers had joined the International Ladies' Garment Workers' Union. In retaliation, they locked out all 500 employees, whereupon the entire work force joined the union, went on strike, and won union recognition.

Unfortunately, their victory was hollow. This sweatshop had no effective fire escape and the stairway doors were kept locked during working hours because "it was difficult to keep track of so many girls." Shortly before the end of the work day on March 25, 1911, a fire erupted; within minutes the whole factory was ablaze. Many workers were confronted with the ghastly choice of being burnt alive or jumping to their deaths. One-hundred-and-forty-six workers died, most of them young girls.

In April 1912 the owners of the company, Max Blanck and Isaac Harris, were put on trial for manslaughter. Three weeks later the jury reached a verdict of not guilty.

The tragedy sent shock waves through the city and the state. Almost immediately, the state legislature set up an investigatory commission to recommend changes in the law. Within three years, three dozen new laws were passed relating to job safety.

The building presently on the site bears a plaque put up by the ILGWU. It simultaneously commemorates the victims' martyrdom and lauds the American Way of Life for since providing "new concepts of social responsibility and labor legislation that have helped make American working conditions the finest in the world." How ironic that 70 years later there are still sweatshops operating within a mile of this spot, and that

"HERE IS THE REAL TRIANGLE."

Illustration by John Sloan.

flagrant safety violations may exist even in union shops. Forty-seven years after the Triangle fire, 24 people died in a factory at 623 Broadway, near Houston Street, a wooden building with no sprinkler system and worthless fire escapes.

On March 12, 1977, more than a thousand women marched from here to Union Square, demonstrating in favor of affirmative action, day-care facilities, abortion rights, and against sterilization abuse.

B11. **The Book Center** *(18 Washington Place, corner of Greene Street)*
This is the NYU Bookstore, scene of a student strike in 1967. *NYU INC.* describes it thus:

> In February, 1967, the NYU Bookstore at the Square was struck over demands to lower prices, improve service, and form a cooperative. Bookstore workers joined student pickets, bringing students and workers together for the first time.

The strike was an important milestone in the politicizing of the campus, providing many students with their first experience in organization, confrontation, and negotiation.

B12. **Courant Institute, Warren Weaver Hall** *(251 Mercer Street, between West 3 and West 4 Streets)*
The Courant Institute is the mathematics and computer science center of New York University. In the 1960s the Atomic Energy Commission helped keep the institute from begging in the streets by giving it $1 million to $2 million a year. Its multimillion-dollar computer, lent to NYU by the AEC, was used by faculty to complete 17 projects for the Pentagon between 1967 and 1969. During the 1970 student strike, 200 members of SDS (Students for a Democratic Society) occupied Courant and held the computer for $100,000 ransom, with which they proposed to provide bail for imprisoned Black Panthers.

In April 1971 striking NYU maintenance workers, members of Teamsters Local 810, formed a picket line around Weaver Hall, which houses the university's heating plant. NYU hired scab truck drivers, accompanied by 200 helmeted and riot-equipped police, to break the line and ultimately the strike.

B13. **Bobst Library** *(70 Washington Square South, between Washington Square East and LaGuardia Place)*
This is the University Library, 12 stories of inner balconies surrounding an airy central atrium. On the tenth floor is the Tamiment Institute Library and Robert F. Wagner Labor Archives, one of the finest collections in the

country for research in labor history and left-wing and radical movements. The Tamiment collection, acquired in 1963, was originally the library of the Rand School of Social Science, a Socialist Party school founded in 1903. The Wagner Archives collects primary trade union material and is cosponsored by Tamiment and the New York City Central Labor Council.

The institute is open to the public, but because access to the rest of Bobst Library is restricted to NYU students and faculty, you will need to get a day pass to visit the institute. Tell the guard what you want and he will direct you to the appropriate office. The institute's hours change seasonally, so call before you go: 598-3708, 598-3709.

B14.   **Loeb Student Center** *(566 LaGuardia Place, at Washington
Square South)*
During the 1960s Loeb served as the command post for large-scale student activism. NYU's participation in the 1970 nationwide student strike began here. As *NYU INC.* notes:

> On the night of May 4, 1970, 1,000 NYU students met in Loeb Student Center. They were angry at the U.S. invasion of Cambodia and stunned by the fresh news of the killings of students by the National Guard at Kent State University. Several students returning from a New Haven rally supporting the Black Panthers presented a call for a national student strike around three demands: end the war now; free all political prisoners; end campus complicity with the war machine. The meeting swiftly ratified a strike at NYU for these demands. Amidst news of a spreading national strike movement, preparations in Loeb continued through the night.
>   . . . The strike lasted until the end of the semester: over three weeks. Regular classes and exams were cancelled. But rather than closing NYU down, the strikers took it over. Large numbers of students and faculty began creating their own intellectual community dedicated to working on *their* problems, not the problems of the Trustees.

Two years earlier, when the South Vietnamese ambassador tried to address a small gathering of the Young Republicans here, members of SDS, with some street people, disrupted the meeting. After lowering the U.S. and South Vietnamese flags, they raised the flag of the National Liberation Front.

Before the construction of the Student Center, this site was occupied by Madame Branchard's, a boarding house that came to be called the "House of Genius." Among those who stayed here were Theodore Dreiser, Upton Sinclair, Eugene O'Neill, and Frank Norris.

B15.   **Judson Memorial Church** *(58 Washington Square South, at*
Thompson Street)
Judson Memorial is an interdenominational church. Like Washington
Square Methodist Church, it has long associated itself with avant-garde and
progressive causes. In the 1960s it sponsored the "Hall of Issues," a weekly
public forum whose topics ranged over the whole spectrum of social and
political issues of the time. Some of its current programs are the Judson
Poets' Theater, the Judson Prostitution Project (whose goal is the
decriminalization of prostitution), and the Center for Medical Consumers
and Health Care Information.

The church itself is a handsome building that has been declared a
national landmark.

B16.   **1 Fifth Avenue** *(near Washington Mews)*
In the first decade of the twentieth century, small houses lined lower Fifth
Avenue. One of those that stood here was occupied by the A Club, an early
version of an urban commune. The radical intellectuals who lived together
here shared expenses and household responsibilities.

In April 1906 Maxim Gorky arrived in the United States, and almost
immediately made his way to the A Club, where he and Mark Twain
organized a campaign to raise funds for Russian revolutionaries. Gorky was
lionized by New Yorkers, although he was so feared by the Russians that
they sent a secret police agent to dog his footsteps. However, when it was
discovered that he was traveling with a woman who was not his wife,
bourgeois morality got the better of revolutionary enthusiasm, and Gorky
and Mme. Andreieva were ostracized by polite society. After being ejected
from three hotels in one day, they finally took refuge at the A Club.

B17.   **11 Fifth Avenue** *(at East 9 Street)*
At different times Washington Irving and Mark Twain lived in one of the
small houses that stood here. This fact is noted on a plaque attached to the
building. Both authors are revered as All-American Folk Heroes, while little
is remembered of their pungent social criticism. To remedy this, we offer
the following:

> ... the almighty dollar,* that great object of universal devotion through-
> out our land, seems to have no genuine devotees in these peculiar
> villages; and unless some of its missionaries penetrate there, and erect
> banking-houses and other pious shrines, there is no knowing how long
> the inhabitants may remain in their present state of contented pov-
> erty....
>   *This phrase, used for the first time in this sketch, has since passed
> into current circulation, and by some has been questioned as savoring of

irreverence. The author, therefore, owes it to his orthodoxy to declare that no irreverence was intended even to the dollar itself; which he is aware is daily becoming more and more an object of worship.

Washington Irving
The Creole Village

Man is the only Patriot. He sets himself apart in his own country, under his own flag, and sneers at the other nations, and keeps multitudinous uniformed assassins on hand at heavy expense to grab slices of other people's countries, and keep *them* from grabbing slices of *his*. And in the intervals between campaigns he washes the blood off his hands and works for "the universal brotherhood of man"—with his mouth.

Mark Twain
The Damned Human Race

In the adjacent house was Mabel Dodge's salon, one of the highlights of pre-World War I bohemian life. Dodge, a wealthy heiress who had lived in Italy, transplanted to New York the European tradition of holding open house once a week. To these evenings came a wide variety of guests: crackpots and dreamers, artists and activists. Among them were many luminaries of the left: Margaret Sanger, the birth-control advocate; Lincoln Steffens, the muckraker; the *Masses* crowd; and Big Bill Haywood and Elizabeth Gurley Flynn, leaders of the Industrial Workers of the World (IWW)—prophets of industrial unionism and the overthrow of capitalism. Many extraordinary ideas were hatched at the Dodge salon and financed with Dodge money. One of these was the Paterson Pageant.

In 1913 an IWW strike at the Paterson, New Jersey, textile mills was failing for lack of funds. When Bill Haywood described the plight of the strikers who had been out for five months, Dodge conceived the idea of dramatizing the strike to raise money. The idea caught fire. John Reed agreed to write and direct a pageant, and got himself arrested in Paterson while gathering material. The strikers loved the idea; 1,000 of them crossed over into New York and marched to Madison Square Garden, which was ablaze with a gigantic sign spelling out IWW. Twenty thousand New Yorkers came to see the dramatic and musical reenactment of the strike. Although the pageant was an artistic success, it was a financial failure. The strikers had no choice but to return to work.

B18.   **18 West 11 Street** *(off Fifth Avenue)*
On March 6, 1970, the house that stood here was destroyed in an explosion in which three people were killed. Two others fled from the wreckage with their clothes in shreds. Although never proved conclusively, it has always

been accepted that the house was a Weather Underground bomb factory. The Weathermen represented that part of the New Left that moved from moral outrage through militant resistance to violence. In a sense, with the explosion on West 11 Street, this nihilist element began to self-destruct.

Cathlyn Wilkerson, one of the survivors and the daughter of the owners of the house, went underground for ten years. In July 1980, when she surfaced and turned herself in to the authorities, she was sentenced to three years for illegal possession of dynamite and criminally negligent homicide. At this writing, Kathy Boudin, the other survivor, is on trial in upstate New York.

Photo by Diane Neumaier

The new house on the site is remarkable for its architecture. Its lower floors appear to have been partially rotated outward, creating the illusion of revealing the building's concealed interior. Those who know the history of the site cannot help but be moved by this odd but somehow appropriate design.

B19.   **Salamagundi Club** *(47 Fifth Avenue, between East 11*
and East 12 Streets)

Salamagundi is an artists' club that occupies part of this stately mansion. It is worth a visit just to see how the other half lived on lower Fifth Avenue. The interior is beautifully maintained and relatively unchanged.

Another part of the building houses the U.S. branch of P.E.N., the international writers' organization, one of whose main concerns is the freedom of writers from harassment and incarceration.

The 1933 international meeting of P.E.N. was held in Yugoslavia, just two weeks after the great ceremonial Burning of the Books of 58 German writers whose politics or genes were anathema to the Nazis. At that meeting, the U.S. delegation introduced a resolution "to prevent the individual centers of the P.E.N. . . . from being used as weapons of propaganda in the defence of persecution inflicted in the name of chauvinism, racial prejudice and political ill-will."

This was the opening round of an anti-Nazi campaign in P.E.N. The organization's historian, Marchette Chute, writes:

> Ernst Toller had been invited to be one of the speakers at the Congress and his name was on the agenda. A very fine playwright, Toller was one of a growing number of writers who were exiles from Germany. He was a Jew, a radical, a former Communist; the German delegation was determined that he should not be permitted to speak.
>
> This attempt to silence Toller was one of the first signs of the deadly creeping movement of the Nazis outside the borders of their own country, and as soon as the question came up, the Congress erupted. . . . [H.G.] Wells, unperturbed by the tumult, put the question to the vote, and it was the will of the majority that Toller be permitted to speak.
>
> There was a frenzy of both hissing and cheering in the little opera house where the meeting was being held, and the German delegation rose and walked out of the building.*

---

*Marchette Chute, *P.E.N. American Center: A History of the First Fifty Years* (New York: P.E.N. American Center, 1972).

Both before and during the war, the U.S. branch played a leading role in support of exiled German writers, such as Toller and Thomas Mann.

B20. **60 Fifth Avenue** (*at West 12 Street*)
Standing behind four useless Greek columns is the luxurious lair of *Forbes* magazine. This self-styled "capitalist tool" regularly grinds out helpful hints on the care and feeding of unearned incomes.

The lobby of the building is something of a shock. Where you would expect to find bare walls or elevator doors, there are cases filled with the memorabilia of tsarist Russia: Fabergé eggs, gilt-framed photographs, imperial currency, and jeweled cigarette holders. When Franklin Delano Roosevelt coined the term "economic royalist," he must have had someone like Malcolm Forbes in mind. Forbes's attachment to the good old days when the "Little Father" had the power of life and death over his peasants makes it obvious what kind of a United States he would like to see. Perhaps one day Forbes's capitalist cufflinks will be mounted in the Museum of the Revolution.

B21. **The New School** (*65 Fifth Avenue, near East 13 Street*)
The New School for Social Research was founded in 1919 by a group of defectors from Columbia University, including Charles Beard and John Dewey, who had resigned in protest at the dismissal of two teachers for their political views. They were determined to set up a school that would have no grades and give no degrees, but would, in the words of John R. Everett, the school's current president, "supply instruction for people who wanted to learn," and "never be in a position of kowtowing to the money boys." The New School was the first college in the country to offer courses in Black culture, under the instruction of no less an authority than Dr. W.E.B. Du Bois (see Lower East Side A6).

A plaque in the lobby of the building explains the origins of the graduate faculty. In 1933, when scholarship became dangerous in Germany, the school opened a "University in Exile," making it possible for "167 imperiled scholars and their families to find safety and intellectual freedom on these shores." As President Everett states it:

> It was agonizingly difficult . . . to bring these professors and their families over in such large numbers because of our own State Department's reluctance at the time to open the doors to refugees. Furthermore, many scholars had to literally be smuggled out of Germany. A man who became dean of The New School's Graduate Faculty, Hans Staudinger, was rescued from a Hamburg jail that Hitler had put him in, where they

had broken both of his legs and were torturing him. Nobody knows who sold what to save him.*

While some of these refugees moved on to other jobs, others remained to form the nucleus of the graduate faculty. The plaque lists these scholars, as well as the corporate, labor, and individual benefactors who made the University in Exile possible.

The New School is still an innovative place, and one can find in the current catalog such courses as "Comparative Socialism," "Radicalism, Reformism, and the Labor Movement," and "American Volunteers in the Spanish Civil War ('Lincoln Brigade')." (For more on the New School, see Greenwich Village A13.)

---

*Lithopinon 26 (New York: Amalgamated Lithographers of America, 1972).

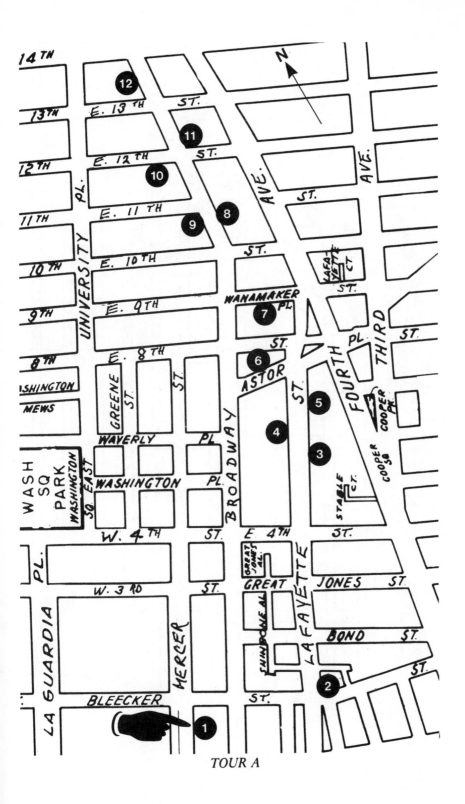

TOUR A

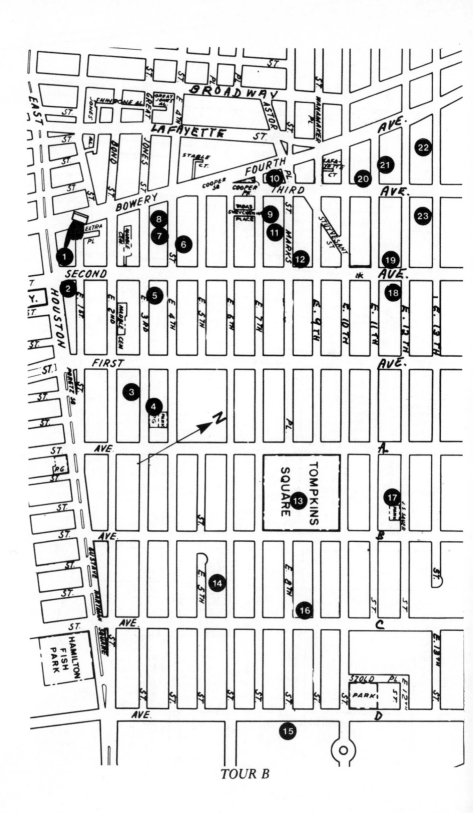

TOUR B

7

The East Village

The hippies came, hitching out of Kansas. Backpacking down from Maine. Jolting along in beat-up buses covered with dayglo sunrises. They had few belongings: a war surplus jacket, a tape recorder with some scratchy cassettes, a hash pipe, maybe some forged I.D. They adopted new names like "Groovy" and "Ladyfinger," and buried their past beneath masses of straggly hair and ill-fitting clothes....

They came to the Lower East Side and became part of the already existing cultural fruit salad: Ukrainian crones in babushkas waddling out of bakery shops, dashikied blacks with new Afros practicing Islamic chants on stoops spread with pieces of carpet, Puerto Rican kids boogeying to bongo drums, black-clothed Hasidic Jews clutching their breasts and scurrying along the sidewalk, mad artists dangling off fire escapes painting the sides of buildings, and vendors dealing grass from hot dog carts. Amidst this urban chaos came the hippies, skipping barefoot through the broken glass, shoving daffodils into your hand, murmuring, "Help is on the way... loose change?... got a joint?"

Abbie Hoffman
Soon to be a Major Motion Picture

Me gustaria que hubieran mas jardines y ningunas drogas. Sueno de mas edificios y arboles en el vecindario.... Quiero que todos dejen de pelear y que todos consigan buen empleo. Deseo que todos podramos ser amigos y que hagamos un mejor lugar para todos en el mundo.

Frank Picon, Edad 10

>I would like to have more gardens and no drugs. I dream about more buildings and trees in the neighborhood.... I want people to stop fighting and everyone to get a good job. I wish that we could all be friends and make a better place for all the people in the world.
>
>*Frank Picon, Age 10*
>From *The Quality of Life in Loisaida, Vol. VI, No. 3*

This area, like most in Manhattan, has experienced many changes of population. Until World War II its people were mostly East European Jews, and its character was much like the section to its south. In fact, the whole district between the Brooklyn Bridge and East 14 Street was called the Lower East Side. After the war, the European immigrants began to be replaced by newcomers from Puerto Rico, who came to call their neighborhood *Loisaida*, creating a Spanish word out of the old name.

At the same time, the high rents in Greenwich Village were sending artists and writers in search of cheaper housing, and they drifted eastward into what they called the East Village. In the 1960s much of the area was taken over by the hippies. The hippie movement is dead, but the East Village still retains the flavor of the counterculture, mingled with that of the Puerto Ricans, Poles, Russians, and Jews. The tenements still stand, dilapidated and decaying but full of life, their people struggling to maintain dignity in the face of grinding poverty and official neglect.

The western part of the area has a much different history. Originally an enclave of the very rich, it became commercial when the Astors and their friends abandoned it, leaving the Astor Library and Cooper Union behind. Recently it has experienced something of a renaissance with the establishment of the Public Theater.

TOUR A   *The Lafayette-Astor Corridor*

Subway information

Start: Spring Street Station (IRT) #6 train
Finish: 14th Street Station (IRT) #6 train

A1.   **Laissez-Faire Books** *(206 Mercer Street, south of Bleecker Street)*
If the name "Laissez-Faire" suggests that this is a right-wing bookstore, you're half-right—it's half-left. Anarchist theory makes for strange bed-

fellows, which accounts for Ayn Rand and Emma Goldman sharing shelf space here. The store stocks many radical books, some of which are not easy to find elsewhere. But, since the anarchists' bête noire is "the state," it does not carry books by Marxists, whose "dictatorship of the proletariat" is anathema to them.

On this block, the African Grove Theater opened in 1821. It was an all-Black troupe that devoted itself to playing Shakespeare and other classics. This was an extraordinarily courageous undertaking, first because most theater at the time was melodrama or cabaret, but even more because it was Black—and slavery was still legal in New York! The company was plagued by white toughs who invaded the theater and disrupted performances. It managed to survive for nearly ten years before the authorities, using typically inverted logic, closed it down to eliminate the disturbances.

A2.   **339 Lafayette Street** *(near Bleecker Street)*
This small building is owned by the War Resisters League. The league came into existence after World War I to protect the rights of conscientious objectors "whose pacifism was secular or political." Since then it has been in the forefront of antiwar and antioppression movements. During the cold war it founded the Pacifica Foundation, now a network of listener-sponsored radio stations including, in New York, WBAI-FM (99.5 on the dial). As early as 1963 the league was agitating for withdrawal of U.S. troops from Vietnam, using tactics such as draft-card burning. In 1969 the league's old offices on Beekman Street were wrecked in a raid during which its mailing lists disappeared, strongly suggesting FBI involvement.

Sharing the cramped space in the "Peace Building" are several other pacifist and radical organizations, among them the A.J. Muste Foundation. Muste was, successively, a Communist, a Trotskyist, and a radical pacifist. He headed both the Brookwood Labor College, which produced a generation of labor left-wingers in the 1930s, and the Fellowship of Reconciliation, which played a leading role in the antiwar movement of the 1960s.

Lest you forget that left-wing enterprises are precarious operations, note the sign on the door to the roof: "Please don't go on the roof—it might cave in."

Lafayette Street is named after the famous French general, who defied an order from his king by coming to these shores to fight in the American Revolution. While his fame is enduring, his stand on slavery is not as well known as it deserves to be: "I would never have drawn my sword in the cause of America if I could have conceived that thereby I was founding a land of slavery."

Photo by Diane Neumaier

A3. **Cityarts** *(417 Lafayette Street, north of East 4 Street)*
This is the organization responsible for inspiring and directing most of the best murals on the walls of New York. Since 1969 Cityarts has been involving neighborhood residents in the planning and execution of these huge works of art; this participation is reflected in the strength of the subject matter and the vigor of the styles.

You are welcome to visit the office, but please call for an appointment; their number is 673-8670. The workers here, while harried, are warm, friendly, and knowledgeable. The office is filled with photographs of finished murals, sketches of proposed ones, and books on mural craftsmanship. In addition, there is a slide show for rent that illustrates the evolution of various murals. If you would like to get a murals movement off the ground in your community, Cityarts offers, for a reasonable fee, technical assistance and the benefit of their experience.

A4. **Colonnade Row** *(428–434 Lafayette Street, south of Astor Place)*
A century and a half ago, this neighborhood would have knocked your socks off. Lafayette Street was Lafayette Place, a short, secluded, tree-lined, super-luxury esplanade developed by and for the mighty Astors and their

like: the Vanderbilts, Delanos, and Schermerhorns. These houses are the last vestiges of that neighborhood.

John Jacob Astor was the king of the robber barons. He started in the musical instrument business, moved from there into furs, then to Oriental trade, and finally into real estate. What with one thing and another, when he died in 1848 he was the richest man in the world. His property holdings, as revealed in his will, are enough to stagger the imagination. By the time of his son's death in 1875, the family real estate holdings read like the city directory. We quote from Harvey O'Connor's book, *The Astors*:

> ... in ledgers and on plat books was recorded a business that drew tribute from every major thoroughfare in the metropolis. There were Astor houses, tenements, business structures, warehouses—every kind of building—to be found on Avenue A and First, Third, Fourth, Fifth, Sixth, Seventh, Eighth, Ninth, Tenth and Eleventh Avenues.
>
> On the numbered streets, east and west, there was Astor property on: Third, Fourth, Fifth, Sixth, Seventh, Eighth, Eleventh, Little West Twelfth, Thirteenth, Fourteenth, Fifteenth, Sixteenth, Seventeenth, Eighteenth, Nineteenth, Twentieth, Twenty-fifth, Twenty-sixth, Twenty-seventh, Twenty-ninth, Thirtieth, Thirty-third, Thirty-fourth, Thirty-fifth, Thirty-sixth, Thirty-ninth, Fortieth, Forty-first, Forty-second, Forty-third, Forty-fourth, Forty-fifth, Forty-sixth, Forty-seventh, Forty-eighth, Forty-ninth, Fiftieth, Fifty-first, Fifty-second, Fifty-fourth, Fifty-fifth, Fifty-sixth, Seventy-fourth, Seventy-fifth, Seventy-sixth, Seventy-ninth, Ninetieth, Ninety-first, Ninety-second, Ninety-third, Ninety-fourth, Ninety-sixth, 107th, 117th, 125th, 129th, 130th, 150th, 185th. On the named streets and avenues: Amsterdam, Barclay, Barrow, Bleecker, Bowery, Duane, Elizabeth, Front, Gansevoort, Grand, Greene, Greenwich, Garrison, Houston, Hudson, John, King, Lafayette, Lenox, Leroy, Liberty, Macomb, Madison, Mercer, Nassau, New, Park, Park Row, Pearl, Pine, Prince, St. Nicholas, South, Vesey, Wall, Washington, West, White, and Worth.

The largest single unit was the entire area between 42 and 51 Streets, from Broadway to the Hudson River.

At the same time that the Astors were living here in luxurious splendor, the area east of Third Avenue was becoming one of the ugliest and most disease-ridden neighborhoods in the city. Much of this tenement property was owned by the Astors, who squeezed the poor dry by charging exorbitant rents. They spent the bare minimum on repairs and did not extend charity to those made ill by the foul living conditions. And to perpetuate this profitable state of affairs, State Senator William Waldorf Astor in 1880 engineered legislation that had the effect of delaying tenement reform for almost two decades. The Astors were New York's pioneer slumlords, setting the standard for future generations.

A5. **Public Theater** *(425 Lafayette Street, south of Astor Place)*
One of John Jacob Astor's minor interests was the endowment of a library.
After his friend James Cogswell had wheedled him into the project, Astor
provided money for the purchase of books, although the old tightwad
stopped short of sacrificing income-producing real estate for the construction of a building to house them. Through Cogswell's efforts the book
collection grew to be the largest in the country, while the library was built
only after Astor's death, via a provision of his will. Eventually the books
here were combined with two other private collections to form the research
branch of the New York Public Library. (In spite of its name, it is not
public; it is independent of the city and run by a private corporation.)

In 1965, when the building was about to be demolished, it was saved
through the efforts of the intrepid Joseph Papp, under whose leadership it
was converted into a multiple theater space now known as the Public
Theater. Here you may in any one evening choose from among several
plays or films, all at reasonable admission fees. (For the first of Papp's
ventures, see Lower East Side A11.)

A6. **13 Astor Place** *(near Lafayette Street)*
One of the perks that accompany the acquisition of riches and real estate is
that lots of places get named after you. Thus, the Astor family has at one
time or another been able to revel in the Astor Hotel, now gone, but once
the largest hotel in the world and the ultimate in elegance; the Hotel
Waldorf-Astoria (Waldorf was the Astor family hometown in Germany);
the entire neighborhood of Astoria, across the East River in Queens; the
Astor Library; Astor House; the Astor Building; and, of course, Astor
Place.

In 1847 Astor Place was graced by the presence of an opera house. But
the brief life and violent demise of this showpiece of the rich cast a shadow
on the name Astor. Just two years after its opening, the opera house was the
scene of a devastating riot, ostensibly caused by rivalry between two
Shakespearean actors: the British William Macready and the American
Edwin Forrest.

Macready was booked to play Macbeth on May 10, 1849. Tension had
begun to build weeks before. On May 9, this handbill appeared:

WORKINGMEN! SHALL AMERICANS OR ENGLISH RULE IN
THIS COUNTRY? The crew of the British steamers have threatened all
Americans who shall dare to appear this night at the ENGLISH
ARISTOCRATIC OPERA HOUSE. WORKINGMEN! FREEMEN!
STAND UP TO YOUR LAWFUL RIGHTS!

On the day of the performance, the police, the audience, and the anti-aristocrats all arrived early. After those with tickets had been admitted, the doors to the opera house were closed and the windows sealed. The crowd outside thereupon armed itself with paving stones and let loose a barrage upon the building. Police, both outside and inside, responded. Inside, meanwhile, a number of the anti-Britishers who had gained entry attempted to storm the stage. Finally, the National Guard was called in, complete with cannon and muskets. When the smoke cleared dozens had been killed or wounded; Astor Place became known as "Massacre Place."

The riot was in part the U.S. working class' response to the European revolutions of 1848 and in part a result of native chauvinism and anti-British sentiments—especially on the part of recent Irish immigrants. The riot and the destruction of the opera house marked the beginning of the end of the neighborhood as an enclave of the rich; they soon began to move away to the safer reaches of 34 Street.

The site of the opera house is now occupied by District 65 of the UAW, AFL-CIO. Most of its members are in the retail and wholesale department store industry. The building is one of the most extensive union headquarters in New York, providing under one roof dental, pharmaceutical, optical, educational, psychological, and social work services. There are also a hiring hall, meeting rooms, offices, and an auditorium.

It is interesting to note that the building is administered by the Tom Mooney Association. Tom Mooney was a labor organizer who was arrested in 1916 and spent 22 years in jail as the result of a frame-up. During all the time he languished there, the left wing of the labor movement agitated for his release, succeeding, finally, in 1939.

One last bit of Astorabilia: down the double staircase at the Astor Place IRT Subway station are some ceramic tiles bearing the Astor trademark: the beaver, symbol of John Jacob's early life as a humble fur merchant.

A7.   Wanamaker Place *(between Broadway and Lafayette Street)*
Although there is no street sign acknowledging it, city maps reveal that the one-block interruption of East 9 Street here is named for the department store magnate, John Wanamaker. It was once flanked by two huge stores, connected to each other by a bridge. To the north, where the nondescript Stewart House apartments now stand, was the second of the great A.T. Stewart Department Stores, built in 1862. (For the first of them, see Civic Center/Lower West Side C7.) Stewart was a prime example of an early capitalist. He said of his employees, "they are simply machines." The "machines" worked a six-day week, 12 hours a day, and could be fired on the spot for lateness, taking long lunches, giving wrong change, or

misaddressing packages. When Wanamaker bought out the Stewart enterprise in 1896, he refined the procedure by hiring women—and paying them less.

The building to the south, still standing, was the Wanamaker Annex, built in 1903. There are 15 floors to the building, but the elevators don't stop at floors six through nine. The *AIA Guide* says they are "used by the federal government today for its own mysterious purposes." The directory says "U.S. Trust Co." The doorman and other personnel aren't talking.

On the ground floor, to your right, are the studios of radio station WEVD. These call letters were chosen in memory of the great socialist leader, Eugene V. Debs. Debs was an extraordinarily popular and charismatic figure. Originally active in the railroad brotherhoods, he became the leader of the American Railway Union. After the disastrous Pullman strike of 1894, Debs was sent to jail, where he became converted to socialism. He ran for president many times as the Socialist Party candidate, twice garnering almost a million votes. His final candidacy was in 1920, when he campaigned from jail, to which he had been sentenced for opposing U.S. participation in World War I.

The radio station was started in 1927, the year after Debs's death. On a grand piano in the reception room sits a bust of Debs; over the piano is a painting that combines his portrait with that of a laborer and with the WEVD microphone. While the station manager told us that the studio is ill-equipped to handle visitors, you might look in for a moment and leave before anyone gets a chance to object. WEVD calls itself "the station that speaks your language." It is the only radio station in New York that offers native-language broadcasts to the diverse ethnic population of the city, with programs in Yiddish, Polish, Hebrew, Portuguese, Greek, Italian, Lithuanian, as well as English.

A8.   Broadway *(at East 11 Street)*
At the beginning of the nineteenth century, when Manhattan was still largely farmland, Henry Brevoort owned a piece of property here. In 1811 the city laid out the lower Manhattan grid, which would have required cutting through Brevoort's land to make 11 Street. Such was his influence with the city aldermen that Brevoort was able to defy the plan, save his private trees, and send traffic on a three-block detour. (The Sephardic Jews were not so fortunate. See Greenwich Village A12.) Grace Church now stands on the Brevoort farm.

A9.   80 East 11 Street *(799 Broadway)*
This building has been occupied by various left groups since the early 1920s, when it housed the offices of the young and vigorous Communist

Party. Charles Ruthenberg, one of its early leaders, lived in the building. The Labor Research Association has been here since it was founded in 1927, and is still active in putting out scholarly analyses of the state of the labor movement.

At present, some of the other organizations whose offices are here include:

The Veterans of the Abraham Lincoln Brigade, those "premature anti-fascists" who fought in Spain in a vain attempt to prevent Franco's accession.

The American Committee for the Protection of the Foreign Born.

Freedomways magazine, a quarterly journal of the Black liberation struggle, which has been in existence since the early 1960s.

Women Strike for Peace, one of the important cogs in the 1960s peace movement.

One of the high points in the history of Women Strike was its turn-the-tables maneuver against HUAC in 1962. From all over the country women converged on the hearings in Washington. As each witness took the stand she was presented with flowers while the entire hearing room stood and applauded. As activist Jeanne Weber wrote:

> Five hundred women grinned when the Committee counsel implied that there was something subversive about a group that had no president and no dues. We laughed out loud when he flourished, as evidence of a plot, one of our innumerable memos proposing a more orderly WSP structure. We howled when the chairman threatened to have a couple of embarrassed guards clear the room. Without really planning it, we had found the most effective weapon against HUAC's smear attack—ridicule.

A10.   **42 East 12 Street** *(between Broadway and University Place)*
In the early 1930s this attractive old building was the home of the Workers' Lab Theater, a pioneering radical theater collective. Many of its members actually lived in the building. The dozen or so who worked full-time in the theater were called the Shock Troupe, and were supported by the small fees they charged. Those who worked at other jobs during the day rehearsed and performed at night, and were called the Evening Troupe. Workers' Lab played at union meetings, demonstrations, and strikes, and often rehearsed on the subways en route to performances, turning rehearsals into unscheduled shows. Performances for strikers and the unemployed were always free of charge.

Photo from authors' private collection
Workers Lab Theater—1932

A11. **Strand Bookstore** *(828 Broadway, corner of East 12th Street)*
Just around the corner, between 8 and 14 Streets, was once the used-book capital of the country—a bibliophile's dream, where you could get lost for a whole day in the dust and must of the old shops. Skyrocketing rents have forced almost all of them to close. The Strand, with the largest collection of used books in the city, is the last of the line, and offers a taste of what Fourth Avenue used to be.

A12. **853 Broadway** *(north of East 13 Street)*
Like 80 East 11 Street (see A9), this building houses many left organizations, including the National Lawyers' Guild and the Center for Constitutional Rights. Both these organizations work to maintain the legal rights of victims of governmental harassment and of women, minorities, and the poor. While they are separate entities, they sometimes collaborate with each other and with other legal organizations. One such case was the recent one involving Judge Bruce Wright.

Judge Wright, a man who understands the problems of minority people entangled in the legal system because he himself is Black, is known for his sensitive treatment of defendants. In one of the cases before him he granted bail to a man accused of having slashed a policeman. The mayor and the majority of the press attacked him, as did the Administrative Judge of the Courts of the State of New York and the Patrolmen's Benevolent Association. The NLG and the CCR joined a coalition of other groups, led by the National Conference of Black Lawyers, to support Judge Wright. When Mayor Koch refused to reappoint him to the criminal court bench, the voters elected him to the civil court, where he is now sitting.

At this address is also the Democratic Socialists of America (formerly Democratic Socialist Organizing Committee), which believes it can institute socialism by way of coalition politics.

TOUR B   St. Mark's Place and Loisaida

<u>Subway information</u>

Start: Second Avenue Station (IND)
F train
Finish: Third Avenue Station (BMT)
LL train

B1.   East Houston Street *(west of Second Avenue)*
Virtually the whole block between Second Avenue and the Bowery is taken up by one of the many lovely gardens in the East Village. These valiant attempts to defy the laws of nature by making the polluted city bloom come in various shapes and sizes. This one is tended by CUANDO; in Spanish this stands for Culturas Unidas Aspiraran Nuestro Destino Original; in English it is rendered Cultural Understanding and Neighborhood Development Organization. CUANDO has built a solar energy wall on the south side of its building, which provides it with some of its heat. Like its garden, CUANDO seems to thrive on adversity.

Derelicts often congregate in front of the garden. They drift over from the Bowery, New York's skid row, where the city's most lost and lonely souls panhandle for nickels and dimes to spend on cheap wine before going to sleep in doorways or, if they have a few cents left over, in a bug-infested flophouse.

B2.   East Houston Street *(east of Second Avenue)*
There is a Cityarts mural here, *Crear Una Sociedad Nueva* (1976). Its theme, the construction of a new community from the old, is an artistic rendering of the CUANDO concept. On one side it portrays the evils of fire, drugs, welfare, and the military-industrial complex; on the other, the hope of the new society: literacy, art, the family, and construction.

Photo by Diane Neumaier

B3. First Houses *(112–138 East 3 Street, between First Avenue Avenue A)*

Although slum housing had been a scandal in New York from the nineteenth century, it wasn't until the Great Depression that serious, large-scale public housing projects were undertaken. This, the first such project in the city (and, indeed, in the country), was completed in 1935. Every third tenement house that stood here was demolished to provide light and air for the remaining pair. Although the initial plan was to renovate the old houses, in the end they were nearly completely rebuilt. Labor was provided under WPA funding and much of the materials was salvaged from the demolition sites. The great need for these houses was demonstrated by the fact that 4,000 families applied for the 120 available apartments.

In back of the houses is a serene, shaded oasis with a children's sand pit and wading pool. The playground sculpture and bas-reliefs are very pleasing to the eye.

B4.　　**P.S. 63** *(East 3 Street, opposite First Houses)*
On the east wall of the school is a powerful mural entitled *Women Hold Up Half the Sky* (1975). The centerpiece is a rendering of the Statue of Liberty enchained by racism, sexism, poverty, and prostitution. Working women climb through her torch and emerge strong from the flame, ready to make a new life. On the side there is a book on which are recorded the names of great women of the past and present, including Rosa Luxemburg, Lolita Lebron, and Sojourner Truth.

B5.　　**The Catholic Worker** *(55 East 3 Street, between First
and Second Avenues)*
Since it began publication at the height of the Great Depression, the *Catholic Worker* has adhered to the ideals of Christianity and the principles of radicalism. Its founder and guiding light, Dorothy Day, set out these beliefs in the very first issue:

> It's time there was a Catholic paper printed for the unemployed.
> 　　The fundamental aim of most radical sheets is the conversion of its readers to radicalism and atheism.
> 　　Is it not possible to be radical and not atheist?
> 　　Is it not possible to protest, to expose, to complain, to point out abuses and demand reforms without desiring the overthrow of religion?
> 　　In an attempt to popularize and make known the encyclicals of the Popes in regard to social justice and the program put forth by the Church for the "reconstruction of the social order," the news sheet, *The Catholic Worker*, is started.

During World War II it opposed fascism while remaining pacifist. Since then the paper has opposed both the cold war and the hot wars in Vietnam and elsewhere. Although Dorothy Day has died, the paper is still very much alive at a penny an issue. (For Day's account of her incarceration for civil disobedience, see Greenwich Village A10.)

While the *Catholic Worker* is published here, a large part of the building, as well as the whole of its House of Hospitality at 36 East 1 Street, is given over to sheltering the poor and the homeless. In an atmosphere of self-effacing goodness, the most wretched of the city's outcasts can find here a bed, a bowl of soup, and a kind word. With an irony typical of the Lower East Side, these gentle souls have of late found themselves sharing the block with Hell's Angels. As you walk here, note the violent graffiti memorializing some Angels who have died.

B6. **Metropolitan Council on Housing** *(77 East 4 Street, near*
Second Avenue)

This powerhouse tenants' advocacy organization has branches all over the
city. At this location it joined with the earlier East Side Tenants Council,
and uses both names.

Met Council offers assistance and advice to individuals and groups in
the never-ending battle between tenants and landlords. It believes in the
necessity for organizing tenants into permanent councils to fight for their
rights, and will go to court and attend hearings on tenants' behalf. It
publishes the newssheet *Tenant*, as well as position papers and information
bulletins. The council staff is almost entirely volunteer and it is funded only
by contributions and membership fees.

This office is open on Tuesdays from 2 P.M. to 5 P.M. for individual
problems and from 6 P.M. to 8 P.M. for group or buildingwide problems.

B7. **64 East 4 Street** *(between Second Avenue and Bowery)*

From the 1890s until after World War I, this building housed a number of
radical organizations. Early on, 't was the location of the *Volkszeitung*, a left-
wing German-language newspaper; at the same time it was a Labor
Lyceum—one of a number of workers' centers that sponsored educational
activities, social gatherings, lectures, and rallies. In the decade before
World War I it was the New York headquarters of the Industrial Workers
of the World: the "One Big Union" that produced an abundance of
militants, poets, and martyrs.

When the Soviet poet Vladimir Mayakovsky came to the United States
in 1925, he gave a reading here. His reaction to this country is summed up
in these words:

> You're an ass, Columbus,
>   yes, I mean it.
> As for me,
>   if I were you,
>   here's what I'd do:
> I would shut America
>   and slightly clean it,
> then I would
>   reopen it anew.*

---

*Vladimir Mayakovsky, *Poems* (Moscow: Progress, 1972).

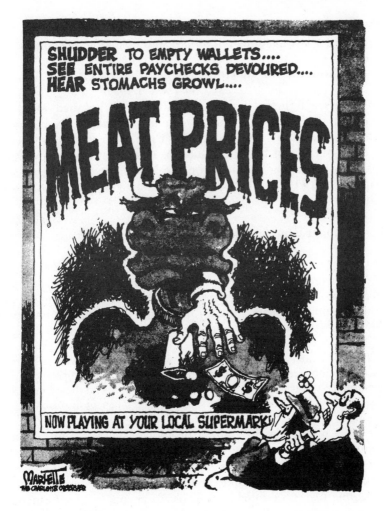

Courtesy of Marlette/The Charlotte Observer/LNS

B8.   **The Good Food Coop** *(58 East 4 Street, between Second Avenue and Bowery)*

Establishing food cooperatives is one way in which the poor have attempted to beat the system (see Lower East Side A10). By buying wholesale and doing pickup and distribution themselves, members can avoid middlemen and keep prices down. The nonprofit, cooperative nature of these endeavors makes them into small communities rather than simply business operations; they tend to develop an atmosphere of goodwill and involvement. The Good Food Coop has signs in its windows (in English and Spanish) that explain its philosophy and operating procedures.

B9.   McSorley's Old Ale House *(15 East 7 Street, east of Third Avenue)*

McSorley's is a beautiful old house, full of dark polished wood, with sawdust on the floor. It is one of the oldest pubs in New York, in continuous operation here since 1854. Until 1970 it also enjoyed the dubious distinction of being a bastion of male exclusivity. However, on August 10 of that year, women won the legal right to enter this sacred sanctuary. You can read all about it in the framed clippings in McSorley's windows.

B10.   Cooper Union *(41 Cooper Square, between Third Avenues)*

Peter Cooper was a rare capitalist: a shrewd businessman and at the same time a man whose intelligence and imagination carried him beyond naked acquisitiveness. He was always more interested in inventing than in buying and selling, and when he made a fortune out of invention and investment, he wished to see that fortune put to good use. Cooper wrote:

> The production of wealth is not the work of any one man, and the acquisition of great fortunes is not possible without the cooperation of multitudes of men; therefore the individuals to whose lot these fortunes fall ... should administer them as trustees for the benefit of society.*

In 1859, inspired by the example of a polytechnical institute in France, he established this school. He wanted to call it The Union, but everyone else insisted on Cooper Union. Free classes were offered to men and women in drawing, engineering, and architecture; a library was opened, and meeting places were made available to anyone with information or ideas to exchange.

Six months after it opened, Abraham Lincoln gave a speech in the Great Hall, sponsored by the Young Men's Republican Union. In it he steered a careful course between radical abolitionism and capitulation to the slavocracy. Lincoln's closely reasoned argumentation, his rhetoric, and, above all, his ability to locate himself in the exact middle of the Republican mainstream, eventually won him the nomination and the presidency.

The Great Hall, because of its large size and its availability to all, quickly became a major forum for intellectual controversy. The greatest

---

The Cooper Union—a Brief History. Brochure published by the Cooper Union, n.d..

movements of the time, and their most brilliant advocates, were heard here: Wendell Phillips on slavery, Victoria Woodhull on women's rights, Jacob Riis on the exploitation of the poor; anarchism, socialism, communism—all were argued from this stage.

One of the most important events to take place here was the memorial to Karl Marx, held on March 20, 1883, less than a week after he died. According to Philip S. Foner, it was

> the outstanding memorial event held anywhere in the world in the weeks immediately following the death of Marx. . . .
>
> What made the Cooper Union meeting in New York so remarkable, was not only its size—in its account *Progress*, organ of the Cigarmakers' Progressive Union of America, called it "The Greatest Demonstration Ever Held in the American Labor Movement in Honor of Any Man"— but the fact that it represented an alliance of different elements who were often at odds with each other but who were ready to abandon their differences in paying tribute to Karl Marx. The meeting brought together for the first time members of socialist and anarchist groups, members of the Knights of Labor and the American Federation of Labor, single-taxers and socialists, and workers of different nationalities and languages.*

Foner quotes a news report from the following day's *New York Sun*:

> If the great hall of Cooper Union had been twice as large as it is, it could not have held the vast throng of workingmen who gathered last evening to do honor to the memory of Dr. Karl Marx. Long before the hour set for the meeting, every seat was taken, and hundreds stood at the door. They went away only when they saw there was no hope of getting within earshot of the speakers. The audience was composed of people of all trades, from all lands—Americans, Germans, Russians, Italians, Bo-hemians, and French. There were many ladies present. . . .

Cooper Union today is a private, tuition-free college of art, architec-ture, and engineering. The Great Hall is still the scene of free concerts and lectures.

B11.   **St. Mark's Place** *(east of Third Avenue)*
In 1911 a group of anarchists founded the Francisco Ferrer Center in a house on the south side of St. Mark's Place. Ferrer was a Spanish anarchist and education innovator. His revolutionary ideas were a threat to both the

---

*Philip S. Foner, ed., *When Karl Marx Died* (New York: International Publishers, 1973)

Photo by Diane Neumaier
East Fourth Street, looking east from the Bowery

Spanish government and the clergy. In 1909 he was accused of involvement in an antimilitary uprising and executed.

Here are Ferrer's own words on education:*

> All the value of education rests in the respect for the physical, intellectual, and moral will of the child. Just as in science no demonstration is possible save by facts, just so there is no real education save that which is exempt from all dogmatism, which leaves to the child itself the direction of its effort, and confines itself to the seconding of its effort. Now, there is nothing easier than to alter this purpose, and nothing harder than to respect it. Education is always imposing, violating, constraining; the real educator is he who can best protect the child against his (the teacher's) own ideas, his peculiar whims; he who can best appeal to the child's own energies.*

---

*Emma Goldman, "Francisco Ferrer and the Modern School", *Anarchism and Other Essays.* (N.Y.: Mother Earth Publishing Association, 1911).

In New York the Lusk Committee, a post-World War I witch-hunting team, attacked Ferrer posthumously. Here is how it characterized the Ferrer Center:*

> ... in the Ferrer or Modern School, run by anarchists until a recent date in the City of New York, children at the most impressionable age were taught an utter disregard for our laws, and imbued with the idea that a state of anarchy was the true blissful state, and that this should be the aim and purpose of the little children who, in all their innocence, believe what their elders tell them.
> That such an institution should have been allowed to exist for almost ten years is not a very high compliment to the City of New York.

Beginning in the mid-1960s, St. Mark's Place was Main Street for the New York counterculture movement. (Some of the more radical called it St. Marx Place.) It was the center of a community whose slogan was "Do Your Own Thing"; whose objective was to live free—materially and emotionally. Rooms were dirt cheap (and often dirty) or you could crash on a friend's floor; furniture could be scavenged from the street, food from restaurants. Used-clothing stores opened, and some gave clothes and food away, along with medical and legal advice. Drugs and beads were sold on the street, and the first head shop in the city was here.

The relationship between the hippies, the police, and the older residents was often tense, and street clashes were common. Sometimes there seemed to be more cops than civilians on the street. And sometimes it seemed that the police were there to pick fights with the long-hairs, rather than keep the peace.

St. Mark's Place is still a lively street, with coffee houses, record shops, a good bookstore (St. Mark's Bookshop at #13), and off-beat clothing and housewares stores occupying the ground floors and basements of the fine old brownstones that were once staid middle-class residences.

B12.   **135 and 137 Second Avenue** *(north of St. Mark's Place)*
The high point of German emigration to the United States came in the decade after the failed Revolution of 1848. One of the revolutionaries who fled to the United States was Oswald Ottendorfer. Here he married Anna Uhl, the owner of the newspaper *Staats-Zeitung.* Together they ran the

Report of the Joint Legislative Committee Investigating Seditious Activities, New York State Senate, Revolutionary Radicalism: Its History, Purpose and Tactics; With an Exposition and Discussion of the Steps Being Taken and Required To Curb It, Part I: Revolutionary and Subversive Movements Abroad and At Home, Volume II; filed April 24, 1920.

enterprise and built the paper into the largest and most influential German-language newspaper in the city.

These two venerable buildings were paid for by the Ottendorfers and erected in 1884, when the neighborhood was predominantly German. What is now the Ottendorfer Branch of the New York Public Library was originally called the Freie Bibliothek und Lesehalle—the free library and reading room. The Stuyvesant Polyclinic at #137 was first called the German Polyklinik. Anti-German feeling was so great during World War I that the name was changed, and then restored after the war. With the rise of the Nazis in the 1930s, the directors thought it prudent to change the name permanently. Directly across the street are the offices of the anticommunist Ukrainian Liberation Front.

(The next five entries are somewhat out of the way, but we believe they are worth the extra walk.)

B13.   **Tompkins Square Park**
This park is named after Daniel D. Tompkins, governor of New York between 1807 and 1817 and then, for two terms, vice-president of the United States. Near the conclusion of his service as governor, he successfully agitated to have the state legislature pass a law providing that, effective July 4, 1827, slavery would be abolished in the state. In addition, he fought for decent treatment of free Blacks and Native Americans and sought to liberalize the criminal code.

Although it is neither as well cared for nor as well used as Washington Square Park (see Greenwich Village B6), Tompkins Square Park offers a bit of green space to the occupants of the decaying tenements of the East Village. While much of it is rundown, with broken benches and bottles everywhere, there are a few bright spots, notably the Cityarts mural on the bandshell and, near it, a striking sculpture carved in bold designs on the trunk of a standing tree. The park's deterioration is probably due in part to its relative isolation from busier areas of the city, but is more likely related to its being in a poverty-stricken neighborhood.

Its location has made the park a natural site for many rallies and meetings. One of these was the "hunger meeting" of January 13, 1874, which was a response to the massive unemployment that followed a severe business panic. It was the largest working-class meeting held in New York up to that time. As the jobless and their families were gathering to hear the mayor present his program for relief, he got cold feet and cancelled the meeting. With the mayor absent, the police declared the gathering an unlawful assembly and attacked the crowd without mercy, injuring hundreds.

During the 1960s, when the East Village was the center of the hippie community, Tompkins Square Park served as its communal living room (and sometime bedroom). The local residents and the cops were not happy with the situation, and there were frequent confrontations. One such occurred on May 30, 1967, when three hippies were hospitalized and 30 arrested in an unprovoked attack by edgy police.

B14. **Sloane Children's Center; Children's Aid Society**
(630 East 6 Street, between Avenue B and Avenue C)

This dark-red, grim building looks like it belongs in a Dickens novel. High up at the point of the roof may be seen the letter *S*. It was built in 1890 as a lodging house and industrial school for homeless boys—a place where these unfortunate children could learn to "make something useful of themselves."

That was in the bad old days; in the good new ones the problems of poverty are the same, but the ways of handling them are a little more gentle. The center runs a crafts program, a playroom, and a summer program.

Just to the east of the center is the Sixth Street Community Center. If you look carefully, you will see that it was once a synagogue and still carries the Star of David. To the west of Sloane is being built the Sixth Street Community Garden, which already has some young trees and raised flower beds.

B15. **Jacob Riis Houses** *(East 6 to East 10 Streets, Avenue D to FDR Drive)*

Jacob Riis was a Danish immigrant who became a reporter for the *New York Sun* in 1877. Moved by the terrible living conditions he saw on the Lower East Side, he produced a series of photo-journalistic exposés that raised public consciousness about the slums. Through his first book, *How the Other Half Lives* (1890), he almost single-handedly effected the razing of Mulberry Bend (see Lower East Side C3).

The Riis houses are noteworthy for the imaginative treatment of their public areas, in contrast to most other housing projects in the city (such as the Lillian Wald Houses immediately to the south). Here we find attractively lighted walkways, benches, and play areas on several levels, and fountains and pools in the summer.

B16. **Plaza Cultural Mural** *(9 Street and Avenue C)*

When we first saw this mural, it had at its base a small park and playground and a sign reading. "La Plaza Cultural de la Communida." The park was built in 1977 by local community organizations and the mural painted by a group of young people of the neighborhood. The mural is still there: a brilliantly colored representation of an African woman, a Puerto Rican farmer, and a Chinese worker. But the park is gone, overgrown with weeds

Jacob Riis Houses

Photo by Diane Neumaier

and strewn with derelict playground equipment; even the sign has been defaced. It is a sad place, a symbol of the never-ending struggle of the poor to create beauty and life around themselves against overwhelming odds.

B17. **El sol Brillante** *(12 Street between Avenues B and C)*
The garden here is thriving, made even more beautiful by the mural on the wall at its rear. The mural was painted in 1978 by a team of young people. It seems to continue the garden into an infinity of rows of growing things, with a brilliant sun rising over miles of fertile fields stretching into the distance.

B18.   **East 12 Street and Second Avenue**
In 1853, somewhere near Tompkins Square Park, Dr. Elizabeth Blackwell opened the first hospital in New York staffed entirely by women and serving women only. It began as a one-room dispensary, the purpose of which was "to provide for poor women the medical advice of competent physicians of their own sex." Blackwell was the first woman to be licensed as a physician in the United States. Her sister Emily, also a doctor, joined her in 1856; together they opened a medical college for women at this intersection in 1868. Subsequently, Elizabeth moved to Britain, where she helped to found the London School of Medicine for Women in 1875. Emily stayed in New York and continued to direct the Women's Medical College until her death in 1910.

B19.   **189 Second Avenue** *(south of East 12 Street)*
For about a half century, beginning in the 1880s, Second Avenue was the "Jewish Rialto." Yiddish theater flourished here, and some of the greatest actresses and actors of the time played everything from musical comedy to Shakespeare in translation. During the 1930s, the Yiddish stage provided much of the talent for the newly emerging radical theater movement. Many whose early lives had been shaped in Second Avenue's vibrant tradition were involved in the establishment of both English- and Yiddish-language companies. Artef was the leading Yiddish group, presenting works by Soviet and American left-wing Yiddish writers. The English-language New Playwrights Theater was organized by Michael Gold and others (see Greenwich Village A5); Stella Adler (whose father Jacob was a renowned Yiddish actor), Morris Carnovsky, and Harold Clurman were among the founders of the Group Theater.

The Group became one of the most significant companies of the decade, igniting the American stage with new plays of powerful insight into the lives of working-class and lower-middle-class heroes and heroines. Its influence has extended into today's theater scene, 40 years after it closed its doors.

With the growing assimilation of the Jews in New York, the popularity of Yiddish theater declined, and many of the theater buildings were demolished. This one, then called the Phoenix Theater, continued to thrive with plays in English. In December 1954 it was the site of the premiere of *Sandhog*, an opera by Earl Robinson, based on a Theodore Dreiser story about the men who risk their lives digging tunnels under rivers.

B20.   **Bargain Spot** *(Unredeemed Pledge, 64 Third Avenue
at East 11 Street)*
At one time, Third Avenue had one of the largest concentrations of pawnshops in the city. Here the poor exchange their last trappings of

respectability for ready cash. When they are unable to redeem their pledges, their precious possessions are put up for sale.

The atmosphere of a pawnshop is unique. The profusion of old and new items and their incongruous juxtaposition on shelves, in cases, or suspended from the ceiling like so many sides of beef must be seen to be believed. Step in, even if you have no wish to buy. If something does strike your fancy, don't be shy about haggling and bargaining in good petit bourgeois fashion. And don't forget: let the buyer beware.

B21.   119 East 11 Street *(near Fourth Avenue)*

This building, once called Webster Hall, was the scene for 40 years of some of the left wing's liveliest and noisiest get-togethers. Before World War I, the *Masses* held annual fund-raising costume balls here, which lasted all night and ended with the celebrants sallying forth into Greenwich Village in full dress (or undress) to greet the sunrise. (For more of the rebels' revels, see the occupation of the Washington Square Arch in Greenwich Village B6.)

After World War II Webster Hall was one of the places at which Peoples Artists held its "hootenannies." Peoples Artists was an organization of progressive performers who also published the magazine *Sing Out!* (which is still going strong). A hootenanny was a kind of radical vaudeville show featuring folk music, stand-up comics, choral singing, and, above all, audience participation. The word "hootenanny" was originally coined on the West Coast during the 1930s to describe rent-raising house parties. In the 1940s and 1950s hootenannies became celebratory events bringing together some of the best talents of the times. During the dark days of the McCarthy period, the hoots were moving expressions of solidarity in the face of adversity, and in many ways anticipated the spirit of the protest movements of the 1960s.

B22.   126–128 East 13th Street *(between Third and Fourth Avenues)*

This century-old building was once a Masonic Hall; the Masonic symbols are still visible on its facade. During the 1872 General Strike for the Eight-Hour Day, it served as the base of operations for the Carpenters' and Joiners' Union. On May 13 the workers meeting here voted to strike and to send emissaries out to nonstriking workers and recalcitrant bosses. In teams of from ten to a hundred, they left, vowing to report back the next day. Their efforts were crowned with success: 400 new workers signed up and 140 bosses gave in, agreeing to continue paying the prevailing wages— $3.50 per day—while reducing the working hours to eight. Flushed with victory and fully aware that spring was the busy season, the workers redoubled their efforts at "moral suasion."

On May 20 parallel meetings were set up. The workers assembled here, while the bosses who hadn't yet come to terms gathered at Cooper Union, a few blocks away. All day messengers shuttled back and forth, carrying proposals and counterproposals. At last the bosses caved in; the workers had achieved the eight-hour day. (For more on the 1872 General Strike, see Civic Center/Lower West Side A5.)

B23.   212 East 13th Street *(near Third Avenue)*
Between 1903 and 1912, the anarchist firebrand Emma Goldman lived in this six-story brownstone. Red Emma was the scourge of the ruling class, travelling all over the country delivering lectures with such titles as "Free Love," "Patriotism—A Menace to Liberty," "Prisons—A Social Crime and a Failure," "The Drama—A Powerful Disseminator of Radical Thought," and, of course, "Anarchism." She left in her wake irate editorials and protest rallies as well as converts, and persisted despite arrests, harassment, threats to her life, and poverty.

Goldman had arrived in the United States as a 17-year-old Russian immigrant, and immediately started working in a sweatshop. After coming upon Johann Most's *Die Freiheit*, she was converted to anarchism, to which she remained dedicated all her life. In 1906 she realized a long-standing ambition, and began publication of *Mother Earth*, a 64-page monthly. During World War I, its content as well as that of her speeches provided the basis for the U.S. government's charges that she had "conspired against the draft." In 1919, after serving two years in prison, she was deported to her homeland during the Red Scare that followed the Russian Revolution.

Here are some excerpts from her writings:*

Anarchism, then, really stands for the liberation of the human mind from the dominion of religion; the liberation of the human body from the dominion of property; liberation from the shackles and restraint of government. Anarchism stands for a social order based on the free grouping of individuals for the purpose of producing real social wealth; an order that will guarantee to every human being free access to the earth and full enjoyment of the necessities of life, according to individual desires, tastes, and inclinations.

Anarchism

Love, the strongest and deepest element in all life, the harbinger of hope, of joy, of ecstasy; love, the defier of all laws, of all conventions; love, the freest, the most powerful moulder of human destiny; how can such an all-compelling force be synonymous with that poor little State and Church-begotten weed, marriage?

Marriage and Love

*Emma Goldman, *Anarchism and Other Essays* (New York: Mother Earth, 1911).

Index

About the Authors

Toby and **Gene Glickman** were born and grew up in New York City. They are musicians, teachers, activists, and folklorists with an abiding passion for un-popular history. They have traveled extensively in the United States, Canada, Eastern and Western Europe. They presently reside in New York, where Gene teaches at Nassau Community College and Toby teaches at the United Nations International School.